LOST LITERATURE #26

A Tradition of Rupture by Alejandra Pizarnik

Published by permission of the author's estate © Myriam Pizarnik, 2019
Selected from *Prosa completa*, ed. Ana Becciu (Barcelona: Lumen, 2012)
English Translation and Commentary © Cole Heinowitz, 2019

Lost Literature Series #26
ISBN 978-1-946433-26-8

Distributed to the trade in the USA by Small Press Distribution
Distributed in Canada by Raincoast Books via Coach House Books

First Edition, First Printing, 2019

Ugly Duckling Presse
The Old American Can Factory
232 Third Street #E-303
Brooklyn, New York 11215

Design and typesetting by Neelufar Franklin and Don't Look Now!
Printed & bound in an edition of 900 by McNaughton & Gunn
Covers printed on paper from French Paper Company
Typeset in Garamond

The translation and publication of this book was supported by a grant
from the New York State Council on the Arts with the support of
Governor Andrew Cuomo and the New York State Legislature.

A Tradition of Rupture

SELECTED CRITICAL WRITINGS OF ALEJANDRA PIZARNIK

Translated by Cole Heinowitz

CONTENTS

TRANSLATOR'S NOTE

SINCE THE PUBLICATION of her debut poetry collection, *La tierra más ajena* [*The Most Foreign Country*] (1955), Alejandra Pizarnik has captivated the imaginations of many of the century's most celebrated Latin American writers, from Roberto Bolaño to Octavio Paz—the latter of whom described her work as exuding "a luminous heat that could burn, smelt, or even vaporize its skeptics." Julio Cortázar characterized "each of Pizarnik's poems [as] the cube of an enormous wheel," and the poet Raúl Zurita praised the piercing clarity with which her poetry "illuminates the abysses of emotional sensitivity, desire, and absence ... presses against our lives and touches the most exposed, fragile, and numb parts of humanity." When César Aira's biography of Pizarnik appeared in 1998, it was no exaggeration for him to state: "There is an aura of almost legendary prestige that surrounds the life and work of Alejandra Pizarnik."

Pizarnik's reputation outside of Latin America has grown dramatically over the last several years, particularly in the English-speaking world. Since 2013, a new collection of her work has appeared almost every year: *A Musical Hell* (New Directions, 2013); *Diana's Tree* (Ugly Duckling Presse, 2014); *Extracting the Stone of Madness: Poems 1962-1972*

(New Directions, 2016); *The Most Foreign Country* (Ugly Duckling Presse, 2017); and *The Galloping Hour: French Poems* (New Directions, 2018). There has been a similar increase in the number of studies and critical appreciations of Pizarnik published in English each year. I have noticed, however, that these essays, articles, and reviews often present a very partial view of Pizarnik and her work, one in which her treatment of sexuality, alterity, childhood, violence, and trauma is framed by her personal struggle with mental illness and her eventual suicide. My hope is that the collection of writings presented here will help to expand this view.

These texts show us the poet at work in the world. We see the breadth of Pizarnik's reading—from Saint John of the Cross to Fernando Pessoa, from Cervantes to Artaud—as well as the depth of her immersion in the avant-garde traditions of Latin America and France. We hear the mordant wit she brought to bear on contemporary social issues (when an interviewer asked if she supported sex education, Pizarnik answered, "Of course—sex is difficult"). But most importantly, perhaps, these writings give us direct access to Pizarnik's reflections on writing. In reading and writing about other authors' work, she examines her own methods and articulates her own principles. In her rare condemnations of others, we learn the strictures she imposed on herself. Conversely, Pizarnik's praise of other writers and the passages she cites by way of evidence often crystallize the essence of her own stance toward writing. This quote from Octavio Paz's *Cuadrivio* in "A Tradition of Rupture" might well have been written to describe this book: "I set out, once again, to interrogate these poems—as one interrogates oneself."

—Cole Heinowitz

A NOTE ON SOURCES

ALL OF THE following texts were translated from the versions published in the Lumen edition of Pizarnik's *Prosa completa* [*Complete Prose*]. We have taken some liberties with formatting the texts for English readers, for example, by moving some of the longer quotations into block quotes. We have also given English translations of all quotations that originally appeared in French. All translations of such quotations are by Cole Heinowitz unless otherwise noted in the commentaries, where the reader will also find the original-language quotations. The commentaries section— located at the end of the book—includes a range of citation, translation, and publication information; each note is listed by order of appearance. We have given the accepted English translations for the titles of essays, stories, and books in the body of the text where Pizarnik used the original French titles; original titles are noted where necessary. The commentaries on each essay begin with information on publication history. Along with the translator's contextualizing commentary and bibliographical references, Pizarnik's own notes are included there and noted as such.

I.

Prologues & Interviews

PROLOGUES FOR AN ANTHOLOGY OF YOUNG ARGENTINE POETS

The Poet and the Poem

> *A poem is a painting with the gift of*
> *voice and a painting is a silent poem.*
> —**Oriental proverb**

POETRY IS WHERE everything happens. Like love, humor, suicide, and every fundamentally subversive act, poetry ignores everything but its own freedom and its own truth. To say "freedom" and "truth" in reference to the world in which we live (or don't live) is to tell a lie. It is not a lie when you attribute those words to poetry: the place where everything is possible.

(...)

In opposition to the feeling of exile, the feeling of perpetual longing, stands the poem—promised land. Every day my poems get shorter: little fires for the one who was lost in a strange land. Within a few lines, I usually find the eyes of someone I know waiting for me; reconciled things, hostile things, things that ceaselessly produce the unknown; and my perpetual thirst, my hunger, my horror. From there the invocation comes, the evocation, the conjuring forth. In terms of inspiration, my belief is completely orthodox, but this in no way restricts me. On the contrary, it allows me to focus on a single poem for a long time. And I do it in a way that recalls, perhaps, the gesture of a painter: I fix the piece of paper to the wall and *contemplate* it; I change words, delete lines. Sometimes, when I delete a word, I imagine another one in its place, but without even knowing its name. Then, while I'm waiting for the one I want, I make a drawing in the empty space that alludes to it. And this drawing is like a summoning ritual. (I would add that my attraction to silence allows me to unite, in spirit, poetry with painting; in that sense, what others might call the privileged moment, I speak of as privileged space.)

(...)

They've been warning us, since time immemorial, that poetry is a mystery. Yet we recognize it: we know where it lies. I believe the question "What does poetry mean to you?" deserves one of two responses: either silence or a book that relates a terrible adventure—the adventure of someone who sets off to question the poem, poetry, the poetic; to embrace the body of the poem; to ascertain its incantatory, electrifying, revolutionary, and consoling power. Some have already told us of this marvelous journey. For myself, at present, *it remains a study*.

The Poem and its Reader

If they ask me *who do you write for*, they're asking about the poem's addressee. The question tacitly assumes such a character exists.

That makes three of us: myself; the poem; the addressee. This accusative triangle demands a bit of examination.

When I finish a poem, I haven't finished it. In truth, I

abandon it and the poem is no longer mine or, more accurately, it barely exists.

After that moment, the ideal triangle depends on the addressee or reader. Only the reader can finish the incomplete poem, recover its multiple meanings, add new ones. *To finish* is the equivalent, here, of giving new meaning, of re-creating.

When I write, I never imagine a reader. Nor does it ever occur to me to consider the fate of what I'm writing. I have never searched for a reader, neither before, nor during, nor after writing the poem. It's because of this, I think, that I've had unforeseen encounters with truly unexpected readers, those who gave me the joy and excitement of knowing I was profoundly understood. To which I'll add a propitious line by Gaston Bachelard:

The poet must create his reader and in no way express common ideas.

ATTEMPT AT A PROLOGUE IN THEIR STYLE, NOT MINE

They are everyone and I am me.

—G.

NOTHING IN SUM. Absolutely nothing. Nothing that doesn't diverge from the everyday track. Life doesn't flow endlessly or uniformly: I don't sleep, I don't work, I don't go for walks, I don't leaf through some new book at random, I write badly or well—badly, I'm sure—driven and faltering. From time to time I lie down on a sofa so I don't look at the sky: indigo or ashen. And why shouldn't the unthinkable— I mean the poem—suddenly emerge? I work night after night. What falls outside my work are golden dispensations, the only ones of any worth. Pen in hand, pen on paper, I write so I don't commit suicide. And our dream of the absolute? Diluted in the daily toil. Or perhaps, through the work, we make that dissolution more refined.

Time passes on. Or, more accurately, we pass on. In the distance, closer every moment, the idea of a sinister task I have to complete: editing my old poems. Focusing my attention on them is the equivalent of returning to a wrong turn when I'm already walking in another direction, no better but certainly different. I try to concentrate on a shapeless book. I don't know if this book of mine actually belongs to me. Forced to read its pages, it seems I'm reading something I wrote without realizing I was another. Could I write the same way now? I'm disappointed, always, when I read one of my old pages. The feeling I experience can't be precisely defined. Fifteen years writing! A pen in my hand since I was fifteen years old. Devotion, passion, fidelity, dedication, certainty that this is the path to salvation (from what?). The years weigh on my shoulders. I couldn't write that way now. Did that poetry contain today's silent, awestruck desperation? It hardly matters. All I want is to be reunited with the ones I was before; the rest I leave to chance.

So many images of death and birth have disappeared. These writings have a curious fate: born from disgrace, they serve, now, as a way to entertain (or not) and to move (or not) other people. Perhaps, after reading them, someone I know will love me a little more. And that would be enough, which is to say a lot.

NOTES FOR AN INTERVIEW

What is the importance of poetry in the world today?

No. 1

WE NEED A place where the impossible becomes possible. It is in the poem, particularly, where the limit of the possible is legitimately transgressed, put at risk.

No. 2

THE POET BRINGS news from the other side. He is the envoy or repository of the forbidden because he induces certain confrontations with the wonders of the world—but also with madness and with death.

Outside the miniscule secret society of poetry lovers, everyone is afraid to recognize that an encounter with the poem could have freed them. Freed them from what? But this too everyone knows.

A WRITING DENSE and filled with dangers due to its excessive transparency—utterly concrete, disproportionately materialist in the way it reveals images originating in the most distant, unknown, and unsuspected [unexpected] inner shadows.

A writing intolerably dense, to the point of suffocation, but made of nothing more than "subtle links" that permit the innocent, equal coexistence of subject and object while eliminating the customary borders separating I, you, he, we, us, them. Alliances, metamorphosis.

My torment is the transfer of images, forged by "the voice's daughter" on the other side, into luminous presences. A transfer I would like to effect with a tense precision that permits me to master chance and compensates me for my absolute submission to "the voice's daughter."

An intense need for poetic truth. She demands that visionary force be simultaneously liberated and maintained, an extraordinary poise in directing this force [and structuring those images].

I don't know whether I'm talking about poetic perfection, freedom, or about love and death.

No. 3
Thursday, December 14, 1964

A WRITING DENSE and filled with dangers due to its excessive transparency. Utterly concrete, even materialist in the way it reveals images originating in the most distant, unknown, and unsuspected inner shadows.

A writing intolerably dense, to the point of suffocation, but made of nothing more than subtle links that permit the innocent, equal coexistence of subject and object while eliminating the customary borders separating I, you, he, we, us, them.

My torment results from the outpouring of images "the voice's daughter" forges on the other side. And from an intense need for poetic truth. A simultaneous double movement: liberating the visionary force and maintaining an extraordinary poise in directing it. I would like to effect this transfer into luminous presence with a tense precision that permits me to master chance and compensates me for my absolute submission to "*my voice's daughter*," be it inspiration or the unconscious.

INTERVIEW FOR *EL PUEBLO*, CÓRDOBA (APRIL 17, 1967)

1

I SHOULD CONFESS that this question—and perhaps others in their interesting questionnaire—is outside my area of expertise, given that I assiduously ignore literary fashions and the term "boom." I read and reread according to my personal preferences, which may or may not randomly coincide with "booming" Spanish American authors. The reason for this disinterest is easily explained: I love literature. Thus, my absolute indifference to certain Argentine authors whose fame prevents a reader from rejecting the evidence offered by their work, that is: authors of something that still hasn't attained the status of a *literary work*. Under these conditions, I couldn't explain what caused the "boom" of the Argentine or the Spanish American book since I didn't have to wait for the dissemination—or the "boom"—of Julio Cortázar's works: I read them on my own, when I was still in high school. The same is true for the works of Borges, Bioy Casares, Olga Orozco, Enrique Molina, Silvina Ocampo, Rulfo, and a few others...

2

I COMPLETELY SUBSCRIBE, word for word, to an extraordinary essay by Jorge Luis Borges which concludes as follows:

"I therefore repeat that we must not be afraid; we must believe that the universe is our birthright and try out every subject; we cannot confine ourselves to what is Argentine in order to be Argentine, because it is either our fate to be Argentine—in which case we will be Argentine no matter what we do—or being Argentine is a mere affectation, a mask.

I believe that if we surrender ourselves to that voluntary dream called artistic creation, we will be Argentine, and we will also be good or adequate writers" ("The Argentine Writer and Tradition," 1964).

3

I DON'T THINK so. A political poem, for instance, is not only a bad poem but also bad politics.

4

IMPROVISATTORI DON'T SATISFY me, which is why I am not going to speak about the urgent problems that economists, sociologists, and politicians know perfectly well. From my own domain—poetic and literary—I discern that evil is called *opportunism*. It is easy to see a growing thirst for fame which inevitably leads to the dead-end street of rivalry. But this also feels alien to me and devoid of any interest. I like the human creature who is committed to his art, his trade, or his occupation. In the literary realm, I associate myself with those who truly commit themselves, in other words, writers who write well instead of badly. And nothing can force me to read those crass pulp writers who fearfully hide behind the historico-political phantoms of their pretended duties, the better to elude the central commitment of every writer—that which Kafka, for example, accepted, and that which Simone de Beauvoir, for example, could not.

8 QUESTIONS FOR WOMEN WRITERS, ACTORS, SCIENTISTS, ARTISTS, SOCIAL WORKERS, AND JOURNALISTS

1

Do you believe that women should have the same rights as men in every sphere?

Women have never had the same rights as men. They must come to have them. I am not the only one to say this. Rimbaud also said it:

> When the endless servitude of woman is broken, when she lives for and by herself, man—heretofore abominable—having given her her release, she too will be a poet! Woman will find some of the unknown! Will her world of ideas differ from ours?—She will find strange, unfathomable, repulsive, delicious things; we will take them, we will understand them.

It is unnecessary to add that the exalted words of the poet constitute a utopian logic. Because nothing frightens them—women or men—so much as change.

2

Do you believe that contemporary society needs a reform and that this would redound to the benefit of women?

I don't believe contemporary society needs *a* reform. I believe it needs a radical change, and it is in this sense that benefits can redound to women.

3

Do you believe sexual education is necessary?

Of course—sex is difficult.

4

Have you encountered impediments in your career due to the fact of being a woman? Did you have to fight? Against what or whom?

Poetry isn't a career; it's one's fate.

Although being a woman does not impede my writing, I believe it is worthwhile to proceed from an exasperated clarity. In this way, I assert that it is a curse to be born a woman, just as it is to be a Jew, to be poor, black, gay, a poet, Argentine, etc., etc. What matters, of course, is what we do with our curses.

5

Do you believe that the laws regulating birth control and abortion should be in the hands of the church and government men or rather in those of women who, despite being the ones directly involved, have had neither a voice nor a vote in matters of such vital concern?

This question refers to an absurd state of affairs. Every person is the owner of his or her own body, and every person controls it to the best of his or her ability and desire. It is the demon of base prohibitions who, girding himself with "moral" lies, has put the laws relating to abortion in the hands of the government or the church. Those laws are immoral—masters of unthinkable cruelty. By way of illustration, I might point to Freud's suggestion that whoever could invent an absolutely infallible form of birth control would become as crucial to humanity as Jesus Christ.

6

Do you support divorce?

Is it possible not to?

7

Where do you see the most urgent problem for women?

Women's struggles don't reside in one single, identifiable problem. In this particular case, as in others, the watchword is still: "Change life."

8

Are you aware of the fight for women's rights in the 19th and 20th centuries? Do you know which were the first countries to recognize them and to what degree?

I ignore these matters.

SOME KEYS TO ALEJANDRA PIZARNIK

MARTHA ISABEL MOIA: In your poems, there are terms I consider *emblematic* and that contribute to the formation of your poems as solitary, illicit domains like the passions of childhood, like the poem, like love, like death. Would you agree with me that terms like *garden*, *forest*, *word*, *silence*, *wandering*, *wind*, *rupture*, and *night* are at once signs and emblems?

ALEJANDRA PIZARNIK: I think that in my poems there are words I repeat incessantly, relentlessly, and mercilessly: the words of childhood, of fears, of death, of the night of bodies. Or, more precisely, the terms you indicate in your question would be signs and emblems.

MIM: Let's start, then, by entering the most pleasant spaces: the garden and the forest.

AP: One of the sentences I'm most haunted by is spoken by the little girl Alice in Wonderland: *"I only came to see the garden."* For Alice and for myself, the garden is the space of encounter or, as Mircea Eliade put it, *the center of the world*. Which suggests this sentence to me: The garden is green in the brain. A sentence of my own that brings me to another one by Gaston Bachelard, which I hope I remember correctly: *The garden of dream-memory, lost in an afterlife of the true past.*

MIM: In terms of your forest, it appears as a synonym for silence. But I sense other meanings. For example, your forest could be an allusion to the forbidden, to the occult.

AP: Why not? But it could also suggest childhood, the body, night.

MIM: Did you ever enter the garden?

AP: Proust, analyzing desire, says that desire doesn't want to be analyzed but satisfied. In other words, I don't want to talk about the garden, I want to see it. Of course, what I'm saying is still puerile since, in this life, we never do what we want to. Which is another reason to want to see the garden, even if it is impossible, especially if it is impossible.

MIM: While you were answering my question, your voice in my memory told me this from one of your poems: *my trade is invoking and exorcizing.**

AP: Among other things, I write so that what I'm afraid of doesn't happen; so that what wounds me doesn't exist; to ward off Evil (*cf.* Kafka). It has been said that the poet is the great therapist. In this sense, the poetic task entails exorcism, invocation, and, beyond that, *healing*. To write a poem is to heal the fundamental wound, the rupture. Because all of us are wounded.

---

* Italicized passages marked with an asterisk refer to poems by Pizarnik.

MIM: Among the various metaphors by which you construct this fundamental wound, I remember, because of how deeply it struck me, the one that in an early poem makes you ask about *the stunned beast dragging itself through my blood.** And I'm almost certain that the wind is one of the principal authors of the wound, since at times it appears in your writings as *the great tormentor*.

AP: I love the wind even if, exactly, my imagination tends to give it ferocious shapes and colors. Battered by the wind, I go through the forest, I wander in search of the garden.

MIM: In the night?

AP: I know little about the night but I unite myself with it. I said it in a poem: *All night I make the night. All night I write. Word by word I write the night.**

MIM: In an early poem, you also unite yourself with silence.

AP: Silence: the only temptation and the greatest promise. But I feel that the *inexhaustible whisper* is always welling up (*For well I know where flows the fount* of wandering language). Which is why I dare to say I don't know if silence exists.

MIM: In a sort of counterpoint with your "I" that joins itself to the night and the one that joins itself to silence, I see "the stranger;" "the silent one in the desert;" "the little traveler;" "my emigrant from herself;" the one who "wanted to enter the keyboard to get inside the music in order to have a homeland." These, your other voices, are the ones that speak of your vocation of wandering, which for me is your true vocation, as you would say.

AP: I think of a line by Trakl: *Man is a stranger on earth.* I believe that, of everyone, the poet is the most foreign. I believe that the only possible dwelling for the poet is the word.

MIM: There is a fear of yours that endangers this dwelling: *not knowing how to name what doesn't exist.*[*] That's when you hide from language.

AP: With an ambiguity I want to clarify: I hide *from* language *inside* language. When something—including nothingness—has a name, it seems less hostile. *Nevertheless, I suspect that the essential is unspeakable.*

MIM: Is that why you look for *figures that appear alive by means of an active language that alludes to them?*[*]

AP: I feel that signs, words, insinuate, allude. This complicated way of feeling language leads me to believe that language cannot express reality, that we can only speak of the obvious. This is the root of my desire to make poems that are terribly exact in spite of my innate surrealism and the fact that I work with the elements of inner shadows. It is this which has characterized my poems.

MIM: Yet you no longer look for that exactitude now.

AP: True; I look for the poem to write itself however it wants to. But I prefer not to speak of *now* because it's scarcely been written.

MIM: In spite of how much you write!

AP: …

MIM: *Not knowing how to name*[*] is related to the concern with finding *some phrase that is entirely yours.*[*] Your book *Works and Nights* is a telling response, since there *your* voices are the ones that speak.

AP: I worked hard on those poems and I should say that in configuring them I configured myself, and I changed. Inside me I had an ideal image of the poem and I managed to achieve it. I know I'm not like anybody (this is a misfortune). That book gave me the happiness of finding freedom in writing. I was free, I had the power to make myself a form as I wished to.

MIM: These fears coexist with the fear of *words that return.*[*] Which ones are those?

AP: It's memory. What happens is I watch the procession of rushing words, and I feel like a spectator, inert and unarmed.

MIM: I find that, in your work, the mirror, the other side, the forbidden zone and its oblivion produce the fear of *being two,*[*] which extends beyond the limits of the *doppelgänger* to include everyone you were.

AP: You're right, it's the fear of all of those that are contending in me. There's a poem by Michaux which says: *I am; I speak to who-I-was and who-I-was speaks to me. (…) One isn't alone in one's skin.*

MIM: Does this happen at any particular moment?

AP: When "my voice's daughter" betrays me.

MIM: According to one of your poems, your most beautiful love was the love of mirrors. Who do you see in them?

AP: I see the other I am. (In truth, I have a certain fear of mirrors.) In some instances, we come together. This almost always happens when I'm writing.

MIM: One night at the circus you recovered *a lost language at the moment the horsemen armed with torches galloped furiously past on their black stallions.** What is that *something similar to the sounds, rushing hot to my heart, of hooves striking sand?**

AP: It's the unfound language I'd like to find.

MIM: Perhaps you've found it in painting?

AP: I like to paint because in painting I find the opportunity to silently allude to the images of my inner shadows. In addition, I'm attracted by the lack of mythomania in the language of painting. Working with words or, more specifically, looking for *my* words, involves a tension that doesn't exist in painting.

MIM: What is it that so attracts you to Rousseau's "The Sleeping Gypsy"?

AP: It's the equivalent of the language of circus horses. I'd like to be able to write something similar to the Customs Agent's "Gypsy" because it contains silence and, at the same time, alludes to grave and luminous things. I'm

33

also exceptionally moved by the work of Bosch, Klee, and Ernst.

MIM: Lastly, I'm curious whether you ever asked yourself the question Octavio Paz poses in his prologue to *The Bow and the Lyre*: *Wouldn't it be better to turn life into poetry than to make poetry out of life?*

AP: I'll respond with one of my most recent poems:

> *I wish I could live solely in ecstasy, making the body of the poem with my own body, rescuing every sentence with my days and weeks, infusing the poem with my breath insofar as every letter of every word has been sacrificed in ceremonies of living.**

II.

Essays & Articles

HUMOR AND POETRY IN JULIO CORTÁZAR'S *CRONOPIOS AND FAMAS*

"HE HAD GIVEN names to each of his two slippers." Of
Lichtenberg, the author of this sentence, Goethe said: "If he
tells a joke it's because there's a hidden problem." A phrase
which Freud, in his turn, elaborated in his famous essay on
the joke—a magnificent essay that does absolutely nothing to help familiarize us (if humor or poetry can in fact be
learned) with the kind of humor employed by contemporary writers, a humor that is metaphysical and almost always
indistinguishable from poetry. (The most important theatrical works that fall under the heading of *the avant-garde*
bear this out.) When Alfred Jarry states: "Then I will kill
everyone in the world and be off," we learn, not that there
is something hidden in Jarry, but rather something rotten—
Hamletically speaking—everywhere.

At present, literary humor proceeds from an overwhelming "realism." Having recognized the absurdity of the
world, it will speak the world's own language: that of the absurd. In other words, it makes an incision in so-called *reality* and gilds the mirror. The spectators laugh at the way Ionesco's creatures tell their stories, but when the show is over
they discuss it in exactly the same way (a language made of
spent word-coins).

THIS WONDERFUL NEW book by Julio Cortázar aligns humor perfectly with poetry. Who are the *famas*? They are Caution; Restraint; Common Sense; the Directress of a Benevolent Society (*for missing mountaineers*); a fat man in a hat; a traveling salesman; a mother-in-law; an uncle; a woman screaming in fear because they gave her a balloon; a hose manufacturer; someone looking at his watch saying: time is money… *And hopes? They're a bunch of suckers* but the *famas** are scared of them. As for the honorable *cronopios*, they are the bearers of a certain organ—almost obsolete in modern man—the organ responsible for seeing and perceiving beauty. As *cronopio* is a more handsome and less equivocal noun than *classic*, thanks to Cortázar we can apply it to the *cronopios avant la lettre*, as much from the past as from the present. Don Quijote and Charlie Parker, Rimbaud and the Archpriest of Hita… and, of course, Cortázar himself would be *cronopios*.

That being said, it just so happens that *a fama had a grandfather clock and every week he wound it VERY CAREFULLY. A cronopio was passing by and, on seeing this, began to laugh*… We understand the *cronopio*'s zen little snicker: what's this about wanting to count time, to cut time up, to sort it into hours, and from hours to make schedules? The chuckler goes home and, playing around, invents another clock: the *artichoke-clock*. Its operation is simple: *whenever he wants to know the time, he tears off a leaf.* But this is merely the first stage of a magnificent initiation: to reach the heart of the artichoke-clock in which *time can no longer be measured, and in the infinite rose-violet of its center the cronopio finds great satisfaction, so he eats it with oil, vinegar, and salt*… It is often said that time devours us, but here a fragile *cronopio* changes the terms. In the first part of the

---

* Italics indicate quotes from Cortázar's *Cronopios and Famas*.

book, entitled "Instruction Manual," we read: *They aren't giving you a watch. You are the gift; they are giving you yourself for the watch's birthday.* In the second part, "Unusual Occupations," one of the tasks of the large, *unusual* family consists in posing a tiger as if it were a model or a bouquet of live-forevers. Minutely described (so minutely it induces vertigo), we ultimately read in the operations of this strange posing something that illuminates the sense and direction of these apparently absurd acts:

> *Posing the tiger contains something of the total encounter, of alignment before an absolute; the balance depends on so little and we pay so high a price for it that the brief instants which follow the posing and which determine its perfection wrench us as if from our own selves, obliterate tigerishness and humanness alike with a single, motionless gesture that is vertigo, pause, and arrival. There is no tiger, no family, no posing. It is impossible to know what there is: a tremor not of this flesh, a central time, a pillar of contact.*

But since no one would believe that the members of this enchanting family spend their entire lives trying to pose a tiger, they also attempt to refine the spoken word:

> *... it suffices to cite the case of my second aunt. Visibly endowed with a derrière of imposing dimensions, we would never have let ourselves succumb to the facile temptation of conventional nicknames; thus, instead of giving her the brutal moniker of Etruscan Amphora, we agreed on the more decent and familiar appellation, Booty. In all cases, we proceed with the same tact...*

One day, thanks to a distant relative who had risen to the rank of minister, everyone—large and small—is employed in a post office whose doleful and discouraging atmosphere they attempt to revitalize. To that end, along with the stamps, they give each customer a balloon, a glass of grappa, and some beef empanadas; they adorn the parcels with plumes so *the name of the recipient (...) appears to have gotten stuck under a swan's wing...*

THE UNLIKELY ACTS of this family have an irresistible humor. At the same time, in my view, the family represents something profoundly tragic: the eruption of the poetic and the marvelous in what we are given to believe is reality. This family, with its obstinate naiveté, decides to concretize poetry's impossible enterprise: to incarnate, transform into action, that which by who knows what error only lives in the pages of books, in songs, in dreams, and in the remotest longings. (The perfection with which Cortázar shapes his tales is marvelous: even the most fantastical presents an architecture as complete and finished as that of a flower or a stone. One might say that Cortázar never leaves randomness to chance.) Let's consider another *occupation: in order to fight against pragmatism and the horrible tendency toward achieving useful ends,* one should *tear a good chunk of hair out of one's head, tie a knot in the middle, and softly let it fall down the drain of the sink.*

The hair's possible or impossible recovery must be the cherished goal of the bereft. To this end, he must doubtlessly devote several years, destroy the plumbing, purchase the apartments on the lower floors in order to pursue his investigations, bribe members of the underworld and explore the sewers of the city with their help, etc., etc. But it is also possible that it might be found *just a few inches from the mouth of the sink...* and that would produce a happiness so great as to oblige him *to practically demand that every conscious schoolmaster encourage his students, from their tenderest infancy, to perform a similar exercise instead of withering their souls with the double rule of three or the sorrows of Cancha Rayada.*

Cortázar's humor unfolds across the entire color spectrum. It is always metaphysical humor, but at times it is black, at others pink, blue, yellow... It is frequently savage, but its tenderness is inexhaustible, often projecting itself far enough to reach fantastic animals (*Guk, the camel non-grata; the bear that walks around in the pipes of the house*), real animals (turtles), and "mechanical animals" (bicycles). He not infrequently combines humor with the fantastic. This is evident, for example, in the case of the *eminent sage*, author of a Roman history in twenty-three volumes, *a shoo-in* for the Nobel Prize to the joy and satisfaction of his country. But then: *sudden dismay*. A *professional bookworm* condemns the omission, in the twenty-three volumes, of a name: *Caracalla*. The sage sequesters himself in his house; he disconnects the phone; he will not answer the call from King Gustavus of Sweden..., but in truth it is someone else who is calling him, someone *who vainly dials the number again and again, cursing in a dead language.*

I spoke of Cortázar's passionate thoroughness and his mastery of the concept of chance. This is due to the fact that few writers know, as he does, how to "see the infinite in a grain of sand." This attitude—and aptitude—all his own reveals itself in every one of his books, and Cortázar himself admirably defines it in the "Instructions for Killing Ants in Rome:" ... *to patiently learn the cipher of every fountain, to hold enamored vigil on moonlit nights...* In this way, he can speak in *full possession of the facts* and move us deeply by describing the vicissitudes of a raindrop clinging to a windowpane. In this way, he can describe, with the same mind-boggling precision, a neighborhood wake in Buenos Aires, a fantastic animal, a painting by Titian, a staircase... This attitude of incorruptibly *enamored vigil* is complemented by his ceaseless rejection of life defined as habit and order: *Refusing that the delicate act of turning a doorknob, that act by* which everything could be transformed, be carried out with the cold efficiency of an everyday reflex. Nothing and no one can shut his eyes. Things are not merely things; dreams are not things; love is not a thing. *To squeeze a teaspoon between one's fingers and feel its metal heartbeat, its suspicious warning.* Because *it hurts so much to deny a teaspoon, deny a door, deny everything that habit licks to a satisfying smoothness.* Whence his constant references to—or his prophecy of—the objects' rebellion; bicycles, for example: How many more years will they tolerate the arbitrary placards of *this world's banks and places of business: VIETATO INTRODURRE BICICLETTE?* So *watch out, managers! Roses are also innocent and sweet, but perhaps you know that in a war of two roses, princes died who were like black bolts of lightning…* The persecuted crickets will also rebel, and sing *with such terrible vengeance that their pendulum clocks will hang themselves in their standing coffins…* The title of one of these stories is another corroboration of what we're saying: "A LITTLE STORY DESIGNED TO ILLUSTRATE THE PRECARIOUS STABILITY IN WHICH WE THINK WE EXIST, OR RATHER, THAT LAWS COULD CEDE GROUND TO EXCEPTIONS, RANDOM EVENTS, OR IMPROBABILITIES, AND I WANT TO SEE YOU THERE." *Historias de cronopios y de famas* exemplarily attests to the subversive nature of humor and poetry, and to how and how much, before the confused web presented as the real world, both of them—poetry and humor—proceed to expose the other side of the story.

VARIOUS ACCOUNTS OF SOUTH AMERICAN EVENTS, PEOPLE, AND THINGS (SIXTEENTH-CENTURY TEXTS)

WITH THE PUBLICATION of this handsome book, Losada commemorates 25 years of continuous operation. This anniversary obliges us to recall that during that entire period, Losada has been one of the organs for disseminating culture and spiritual values that has most enriched our knowledge of the most diverse authors.

*...a book (of) documents that reveal the tragic grandeur of the early days of what would become these nations of South America...** writes Mr. Gonzalo Losada in his prologue to *Various Accounts...* Alberto M. Salas, the author of several books of great historical and literary importance, and Andrés Ramón Vázquez, head of the press's technical department, were in charge of the document selection. They also edited the notes that introduce—and enrich—each text.

There is no shortage of books dealing with the events of the conquest but in *Various Accounts...* those events are narrated *in the voice of the protagonists*, as Mr. Losada notes. What is fascinating about this *voice* is the passion and

---

* Italics indicate quotes from *Various Accounts of South American Events, People, and Things.*

45

ingenuousness it reveals. In it, one also catches the inimitable zest of adventure, which finds its most fitting tone in the testimony of those who directly experienced it.

Various Accounts... brings together twenty-five texts which, as the editors phrase it, are representative of *forms of life, ways of being; actions and circumstances particular to the period in which the country and its cities were born. A sort of inventory, description, and enumeration of the land, its elements and scenery, and of men, their feelings and behavior...* By means of these testimonies we can therefore *see, up close,* the men who are commonly only names scattered across the pages of history books: Pedro de Mendoza, Juan Díaz de Solís, Martín Domínguez de Irala, Álvar Núñez Cabeza de Vaca—the latter of whose kindness, sense of justice, and delicate, abiding respect for both the Indians and his own people constitutes a bright spot in the dark atmosphere of conflicts and betrayals exemplified by the treacherous murder of Juan Osorio, the only consolation for which is the compassion of Juan Pacheco. Other men also appear, of whom we knew nothing, but who take shape and come to life through one of their letters which, chancing to be saved, allows us to take part in their suffering and woes. Such are the letters of the crossbowman Bartolomé García, of Mrs. Isabel de Guevara, and of the bachelor Domingo Martínez, written with no other object than the need to redress a state of affairs they find unjust. In addition, there are descriptions of islands with their flora and fauna, curious lists of goods, chronicles of expeditions in which they even go so far as to mention the existence of a tribe of Amazons, Irala's astonishing last will and testament, Ambrosio Eusebio's letter to none other than Pietro Aretino... These texts, and many others, grant us intimate access to the peculiar rhythm of life for the first Spaniards to arrive in our lands, and to familiarize ourselves with both their greatness and their wretchedness.

I would not want to omit from this note the deliciously comic quality of several passages found throughout this book. It is, no doubt, an involuntary humor on the part of the authors, but that same lack of intentionality accentuates the comedic power of entries such as the following:

> *Such cunning bitches are they* (the Indians) *that they appeared to be making signs of peace while privately flattering themselves with the prospect of a nice little reception; and when they saw the guests in the distance, the brutes began licking their lips.*

> *...they* (the Indians) *had a great fear of the horses and begged the Governor to tell them not to get angry...*

> *One day, all of a sudden, we saw on the shores of the harbor a man of gigantic stature, naked, dancing, singing, and throwing dust on his head.*

Pigafetta recounts that the captain held up a mirror in front of this same Indian: *And on seeing his face he was terrified and jumped back, trampling three or four of our men.* Another observation by Pigafetta reveals the sad social state of the Patagonian woman: *...the men rapidly took up their bows, and their women, loaded like asses, carried the rest.* The anatomical structure of these Indian women also leaves much to be desired: *When we saw them we were dumbfounded. Their breasts hang down to their elbows...* He further observes the lack of seasoning in indigenous dishes: *They ate mice without even skinning them.*

The same innocence presides over the construction of highly poetic expressions which casually appear in certain texts:

> *A snail and inside it a little piece of coral that seems to have grown there.*

> *...tightly imprisoned nuts...*

> *...we all thought and talked about the narrow-mindedness of everyone around us.*

> *...with tightly clutched sword I descended to test how deep the river ran...*

> *...there are many large pine forests in that land and the pines are so big that even four men together, with arms outstretched, can't embrace one...*

And this indication at the foot of the page: *See angel water.*

But it is above all in relating the starvation they suffered that these voices achieve that intensity which only lived suffering confers on what is said. Before these the reader trembles but also gains an unparalleled vision of the tremendous privations involved in the Conquest:

> *...searching for herbs, regardless of what kind, for we cared not whether they were good or bad, and the man who could catch a snake or a serpent in his hands and kill it thought he himself better provisioned than the King...*

> *...and as the armada arrived in the port of Buenos Ayres with fifteen hundred men, and without provisions, the hunger was such that at the end of three months one thousand were dead; not even the famine of Jerusalem can equal it...*

Obviously no other famine can equal it—*one Spaniard even ate his own brother, who had died,* as Ulrico Schmidl tells the story and as it is sung by Luis de Ramírez: *The things they saw there / have never been seen in writing: / eating your brother's very offal.* This is why it is so disturbing to read the entries for tableware in the list of Pedro de Mendoza's goods. *And so many knives and forks to set what master's table? Were they for carving air?* the authors of the selection ask in their preliminary note.

The reasons for continuing to write about this magnificent book have in no way been exhausted. But faced with the material impossibility of further elaboration, we must hasten to recommend it in the certainty that readers will thank Losada, Mr. Gonzalo Losada, and Messrs. Alberto M. Salas and Andrés R. Vázquez for this anniversary gift.

SILENCES IN MOTION

ALL TWENTY-THREE POEMS in this book have the same fragmentary structure: sets of short sentences followed by silences that occur with the same frequency as the sentences; themes that dissolve—fragments of realities and unrealities that come and go in rapid alternation. This musical transience of meaning is the plot of every poem: metaphysical concepts, solitary objects, and lyrical images interweave, crystalizing at moments to make way for a brief silence which, in its turn, makes way for a new sentence or set of sentences.

Allusive, reticent, mistrustful, stealthy poems. They are constantly speaking of something which seems to be spoken about somewhere else. This elsewhere is the invisible, haunting interior of the poem, and it would appear that the "visible" poem is formed by certain wisps or fibers gathered from this other interior poem. It is as if one were to play a melody—on the piano, let's say—with perfectly discrete sounds and silences, a melody which is simultaneously being played, but without the silences, inside the piano. The poem "Life Towards Everything" offers a more useful example: *in the cypress / our hand touches / the* *sleepless cypress / beneath the cypress.*[*]

In this way, metaphors unfold, questions no one answers, mental landscapes, definitions, lamentations, execrations, encomiums, expressed by an I who at times is a you or a we. They are poems made of meanings and silences in motion; their rhythm alternately evokes two fundamental gestures: concord and estrangement. But then this is precisely what *The Demon of Harmony* is about.

The poem "Central Work" depicts a moment exalted in time, a privileged moment. Suffused with a kind of primordial energy, all opposition ceases in such moments. The possible bursts in like a sun and words become the true ones once again, the ones "not lost in foreignness." By that same token, the painful limit of things is reversed and, consequently, the poet's freedom becomes unlimited. The poem thus concludes: *So that they understand / the terrifying bliss / of any ship / before every shipwreck.* These lines express the highest form of joy. They invoke death, but here death is no longer the unknown that inspires fear, no longer the opposite of life—and one understands how its fascination could be irresistible.

Even though Murena finds the right words to express these things, his tone is furtive, as though he feared—with good reason—that words would calcify the exalted moment his words consecrate. For Murena, moreover, *every term / is an opportunity / for life or death.* It thus becomes necessary to protect both the word and the silence from which it emerges (*do not fill it / do not empty it*), for by expecting everything from words one is likely to end up with faith in nothing but silence: *He who knows / is silent / and he / who does not know / speaks.* It is terrible for a poet to say such a thing. So why does he say it? The perfect response is the

---

one Diotima gives to Hyperion: "By wishing for a world, you have everything and nothing." Incidentally, this astonishing sentence helps clarify the *terrifying bliss / of any ship / before every shipwreck*.) Another poem that brings us close to Hölderlin is "Celestial Breath," in which Murena refers to a total language—that of the *sleepless cypress*, that of the unbroken melody—which doubtless was ours in a past more real than the one described in history books: *to speak with silence, / a sacred loss.* In our exalted moments, we recover that language. Yet Murena knows that it is not only impossible to seek out those moments—since a search entails a means and an end—but also that there are enemies that prevent one from even trying. Not those famous enemies of the soul, but rather these: chaotic chatter and sterile silence (in other words, what generally constitutes our being, day after day, and what we tend—quite unjustly—to call our "inner life"). The realization that *everything is something else* is the only one that effectively destroys such enemies. *A different dimension* or the other side of the story, this otherness admits us to a moment in which now is always (*before never was*) and a space synonymous with *the source / at the center.* A melody, a creature that has become a beloved presence, a gesture of tenderness or compassion, a favorite landscape: so many things can come to be agents of an unexpected rebirth, of a return to an earlier day when nothing could be simpler than discovering "the infinite in a grain of sand." A day, likewise, when the body of the beloved will have the power to change the world: *The nude woman / reclining / with a river / of roses / between her legs /the fabled heron / whose landing / reorders the forest…*

Acts of love—and all exalted moments—*have no name, / they retain / their diamond song.* It is significant that Murena appeals to a stone to characterize the "expression" of these consummate moments. With this, he affirms that no words will ever be able to translate that song. And, in truth, what could you possibly call that which *has no name* and which calls to us in such a mysterious, unexpected way? In another poem, he says: *against the black / earthly garden / the final secret / glows*. To discover—by naming—that secret appears to be the sole province of poetry. Or not to discover that secret, but rather to attempt to discover it. Even if it is impossible. Especially if it is impossible.

Though well aware of the magnificent failure such an endeavor entails, Murena never stops trying to name the other cypress, never stops recalling *the forgotten / song of wholeness*. This is because *a natal voice* still lives *behind a closed / door* inside of him. "And the voice brings us to the country where our origins lie," says Heidegger in his poem "Voice of the Road."

MURENA HIMSELF DOES not isolate the exalted moment. Rather, those moments emerge and disengage themselves from the framework of utilitarian time—an abstract temporal series from which the pure present, pure presence, arises. As for that ashen wall on which someone occasionally manages to inscribe the poem of fire, Murena variously terms it the *meantime*, the *outside*, the *unknown*. Hostile, lurking figures populate this savage place; vigilance, self-protection, and endurance are essential there. *In the meantime, / irony, mastiffs...* In naming the sphere of chaotic chatter, Murena's words become a kind of underground monologue: *son of man, / stem the tide, / cloak yourself in night, / the best thing for you / is to never have been born, / never taken root*. There are two occasions, however, when Murena is plunged into utter dissonance. (A voice was murmuring its "negative theology" via corresponding moans when, suddenly, without knowing when or how, it was abducted by the demon of dissonance.) The voice bristles and lashes out: *Fetus of darkness / thrown into asymmetry, / you know what I'm saying, / age of lead!* The voice cries out: *howl! / howl louder!* These examples reveal a Murena whom meanings get the better of. Yes, he says what he wanted to say, but at the cost of the poetry, which he sacrifices. Nothing could be further from these examples than those beautiful phrases (quoted above) glorifying the forest transformed by the presence of a woman's body. Yet it is no accident that those failed lines should be dedicated to the *meantime*, to the place of *wasted life*, or simply to compounding the mistake. And one of their principle features is precisely this sense of mistake: *History is / a ruined temple / filled with corpses / mistakenly beheaded.* That *everything is something else*, which was the watchword for entry into genuine life, becomes the ironic proof of a miserable trick: *You wait by night / day comes, / you wait by day, / night comes.*

THE POEM "LIFE Towards Everything" commemorates *the plenitude / clothed in the present.* Each set of lines is sustained by the lovely particle *Yes* inserted in the silence. The final lines, however, ask: *But who, / who invented / the human heart.* Everything bore the *same color / as always* and here we have the human heart, the great inhibitor. In "Incipient Poem" he makes reference to *tainted memory* and in "Book of the Storm," he execrates the psyche *(and the psyche's feats / are obscene doodles / on the walls of a urinal).* A hasty reader will think of the split implied between the self and the world (or its equivalent, the split between poetry and the world), and will determine that our author aspires to dwell among the angels. Nothing of the sort, for they too are discredited. One poem evokes *a song of angels / grown old* and in another, though *an angel sets forth / what is just*, he does so *on a big red clock / that tolls the hours / wrong.* What we are dealing with are old, disoriented angels.

That said, if the psyche is the den of obscenity, if memory betrays and the heart is an impediment, if the angels themselves have lost their clarity and freshness, then what? What remains, in spite of everything, is *a ceaseless force, / an inexorable tenderness*, the only kind that will be able to destroy that *nobody in mourning* which separates the parts of the dialogue *(but in the middle / nobody comes in mourning / and sits down)*. It is the ever-open possibility of love, that is, of losing oneself—of finding oneself—in the other. Encrypted in this communion, Murena sees the fate of our solitude, which will be either desolate or joyous according to our *capacity for love*, as solitude *means / whatever you want / dearly*. And what is more, that communion not only determines the nature of our solitude, it also assures the most beautiful permanence: *But those / whom once / we truly love / are forever / inside us.*

NOTHING IS MORE common in modern poetry than this oscillation—or contradiction—which Baudelaire expressed as no one else: "The horror of life and the ecstasy of life." In *The Demon of Harmony*, when everything seems to enclose itself in silence and obscurity, a promise or the fragment of a promise emerges. But the opposite also happens: *The opportunity passed / it has always / passed.* Like a Messiah heralded by Kafka, not only has the opportunity already passed, it never came. Amid bleak rationales and reasons, man roams the unknown. Yet this book tells us that poetry, among other things, *incinerates reasons*—poetry, "who knows the void better than the dead."

WHEN THE ATTENTIVE reader has finished reading *The Demon of Harmony*, when he has already deciphered it (the great problem of almost all modern poetry: how does one penetrate the symbols every poet forges in solitude?), when he has recreated in himself that struggle between concord and estrangement, when, in short, he can reread—but now with his heart, now openly—this by no means easy book, he then feels a very particular emotion towards certain humble lines, for example: *it is yours / my hand...*, which signify much more than a declaration of love. Rather, they are the perfect formula for a reconciliation, or the felicitous truce that is finally granted to one who contended with desperate and inescapable necessity.

ALBERTO GIRRI'S *THE EYE*

Where past and future are gathered…
—T. S. **Eliot**

…where (…) the past and the future
(…) are no longer perceived as contraries.
—A. **Breton**

MANY POEMS IN *The Eye* invoke a human creature riven by duality. It is no accident that one poem is titled "Res Cogitans" and another "Res Extensa." After the creature's leap, during his fall to earth, the first poem says *they are not leaps / that mark his fragile / laborious gait / but rather options, the intimate, / parallel self-projection of disputes. /…**

The poem "Endless, Time" describes the alternation of contraries: *where the beginning of contraction / perpetually follows / peak extension / …*

Of the many poems that signify the contention of opposites, the one in which wakefulness confronts sleep is perfectly desperate and beautiful: *like he (…) who sleeps hungry, / and believes he eats, / and finds himself thirst-tired, / like he who sleeps thirsty, / and believes he drinks, / …*

---

* Italics indicate quotes from Girri's *The Eye*.

By contrast, in "Res Extensa," the bondage to options changes into a harmonious perception of binary rhythm. Each stanza opens with a verb expressing assent: *You know yourself; You accept; You welcome.* Docile, perhaps ironically so, a *yes* is pronounced in time with the changing of the seasons, in time with the phenomena of nature, with that which persuades the living that to be born is to die and to die is to be born. The reconciliation is evident in this fitting image: *the hand / that plucks the petals from your love of life / confusing itself with the hand / that frees you from this life / ...*

With the exception of this poem, in all the others the reconciliation of contraries is only possible *when the idea of the I recedes.* More than a reconciliation, it is a mutual negation: *Neither death nor not death.* By ignoring *how to say: I am,* ignorance is destroyed. *Before I did; now I comprehend.* By ignoring *how to say: I am,* time—that synonym for death—disappears, and there is a return to the original time in which *we were / one and unity and embrace: a verb / without tenses / enters the thing I call / my person.*

Then, when the eye is cleansed of *remains, depository / of the crow's ancient voice,* the eye will behold beauty: ...*and it will behold beauty / after the soul / has itself become beauty. / ...*

In condemning the separation that characterizes the western spirit, Girri attests to a nostalgia common to the greatest contemporary poets, from the wildly inspired to the absolutely lucid: nostalgia for unity and the abolition of time.

HERE, THOUGH COMPLETELY transformed, the old lament is raised: "as with leaves, so with the lives of men." The traditionalism of such themes only accentuates the originality of Alberto Girri, whose poetic journey is among the most solitary. The poem "Relationships and Oppositions," whose subject is love, or rather the couple, persuasively testifies to this originality. This exceedingly beautiful poem comes as a shock to the reader steeped in the western poetic tradition (it not only shocks, it also causes pain, as it is always terrible to suddenly find, transformed into poetry, truths that earlier poets never prepared us to consider as lyric material). It is worth pausing to recall that, despite the vertiginous distances that separate contemporary poetry from the poetry of the past, the theme of romantic love has been preserved and, in a certain way—in many ways—, is still rooted in the conception of love created by the Troubadours. Even in the remarkable erotic poetry of the surrealists, the beloved is usually a kind of marvelous object before which the poet reverently kneels. ("I stand before this feminine land / Like a child before the fire." Éluard.) In other words, the beloved is the lover's means of transcendence. In "Relationships and Oppositions," there is neither a beloved-object nor a lover-subject: there are two people who love each other and, later on, two people who betray their love in equal measure. Before love, both she and he were *bound to the immutable / to their own umbilical cords.* One of the many things that happens when two people love each other is liberation: the *immutable* dissolves in *fusion.* But as soon as *fusion and perfection* no longer hold sway over the lovers, the two, *he and she / perjurers both,* recover the ties that bind them and return to their condition as isolated creatures, separate, "discontinuous."

> *Every word being an idea...*
> **—Rimbaud**

IN GIRRI, THERE exists a "bitter knowledge" which drives him to repudiate all feeling. The tension of his poetic language is nothing if not the materialization of a relentless spiritual tension. Faced with his most structurally rigorous

poems one wonders: Might such extreme order and poetic unity perhaps conceal a contest of oppositions which,
though forcibly subdued, could divert the poems' steady,
even course at any moment? Upon what false bottom are his
phrases built? I believe the answer is: nothing is concealed
in these poems, not even a false bottom. And if at times
a contest of oppositions exists, it exists as a concept—as a
truth—that Girri makes evident through the unity of images in which words and ideas are never at odds. Here, whatever the poem wants to say, it says. To describe contraries is
not the same thing as to write contradictorily. Furthermore,
as was previously stated, the description of contraries is
complemented by the description of encounters with *fusion
and perfection*. In general, we are accustomed to poetry that
has—so to speak—an aura, an underlying essence. In Girri,
by contrast, we find a complete absorption in language.
And this creates a new way of reading in which the totality
of the poem is contained in the word by a kind of horizontal
threshold which nothing is allowed to cross. It follows from
this analysis, not only that Girri is *not* an obscure poet—as
has been said—but that he is in fact *too* clear, which is precisely why he might appear obscure. Even so, I am obliged
to confess that there are two extraordinarily haunting lines
in *The Eye* which I still don't understand: *in the depth, not in
the dark, / in the depth, which is not darkness*.

Doubtless, there is a pleasure in not understanding certain lines in a book of poems; we enjoy repeating them to
ourselves as this repetition mysteriously connects us with
the pure sonority of language. And by repeating them often, their meaning eventually bursts into our spirit, just as
that great master of obscurity, G. M. Hopkins, would have
wished.

ACCORDING TO AN old saying, a poem is a painting endowed with speech and a painting is a silent poem. Concurring with this, Girri makes the paintings of Breughel speak and think in his poem—to my mind the most beautiful in the book—entitled "Exercises with Breughel."

The poet pays tribute to *the visionary generosity* of this Flemish painter who never allowed his *moral passion* to impose itself between his gaze and the outside world. Once again, duality is transcended: in the paintings of Breughel, Girri says, *no distinction exists / between innocent and guilty.* His *visionary generosity* enables him to offer the most crystalline testimony to that which is, to that which exists:

> *it would never occur to him*
> *to condemn an act as such,*
> *be it that of the beggar seeking alms,*
> *that of the soldier*
> *dragging Simón Cireneo,*
> *the masses listening to the Baptist*
> *and asking themselves*
> *why they're the ones listening*
> *and the Baptist the one speaking;*
> *be it the blind leading the blind,*
> *or the triumph of death*
> *in the whines of a starving hound*
> *the parched mouths,*
> *the trembling hands, the dense*
> *intense music of the final second*
> *by which wordlessly*
> *they touch in the dying*
> *their own, identical sentence.*

What characterizes and unites all the figures that populate these paintings is fidelity to what they are (... *none conceive of acting / in opposition to their stigma...*). Each one is presented with his crime and almost all have a crime to display (not even nature is spared: *the crime of snow, / in covering carts and pastures*). Such fidelity allows them to await death impassively. He who is faithful is just and / *among the just / death is a simulacrum.* And if death has lost its reality for the faithful and just in Breughel, they can no longer be tormented by the *imperious doubt of Nicodemus: / given that death / is movement / toward the great void, / how can one die / and return to the womb?, die / and be reborn?, how can these things be?*

It doesn't matter whether the doubt is that of Nicodemus. What matters is *the unusual charge* of Girri's line, which allows three questions to transmit a particular vibration to the reader, a vibration which is often the only guarantee of genuine poetic communication—or more accurately, communion. This is true for the entire book: the "nuptial bond" between word and idea enables the same bond to form between the reader and the poem.

Many of the pieces in *The Eye* have an interrogative structure. Girri poses numerous questions through his poems. This is as it should be. It is not true that poetry resolves enigmas. Nothing resolves enigmas. But to formulate them by way of the poem—as Girri does—is to unveil them, to disclose them. Only in this way can poetic inquiry become an answer: if we are willing to risk that the answer may be a question.

A RICARDO MOLINARI ANTHOLOGY

In *Day, Time, Clouds*, Argentina's most celebrated poet, Ricardo Molinari, presents a selection of poems written over the course of 33 years, from 1927 to 1960. It makes sense to divide this span of time into two parts: the poems written between 1927 and 1945 are those of an excellent poet, while those written after 1945—some of which are merely pleasant, others of which are mediocre, and all of which are superfluous—are those of a poet who has outlived his time and tries to imitate himself.

The first half of the book is thus the more appealing one. Together with the apt, spontaneous cohesion of images and ideas, the rhythm of Molinari's language is very seductive—few others have distilled such subtle music from the Spanish language. Nevertheless, in those poems one catches glimpses of the dangers that threatened, and eventually defeated him: firstly, poetic inattention; and secondly, the inflation of form at the expense of meaning. Take, for instance, one of the poems from 1927—a poem dedicated to poetry and replete with lovely images in the tradition of Góngora: *musician listening in the wind / and in the accident at sea / rock or frothy shore, / friendship never* *sullied / not even a squall / for the child sailor.*[*]

It is still revealing that, already in 1927, the poem poeticizing poetry dispenses with meaning, or rather, its meaning is so trivial that we can dispense with it.

But the defects matter little in these early poems so full of light, color, levity, and grace. Conversely, they matter a great deal when the poems' outward charm begins to tire the poet as much as the reader.

A Wandering Poet

MOLINARI APPEARS IN his poems as a wanderer. On the banks of rivers, exposed to the winds, or standing before landscapes now desolate, now joyful, he finds it impossible to step outside himself, and even more inconceivable to look within. The wind, the river, the flower, the cloud, and the day all grieve or rejoice in accord with the mental state of the wanderer who looks on them with eyes that see only himself, only the absence of himself. His contact with the world is very slight, but the suffering caused by that minimal contact is disproportionately great, and in this way, at times, communication is established with the reader: through lack, through the beautifully communicated impossibility of communicating.

Poetry without presence. No one and nothing exists. Only a highly gratifying rhythm—in his best poems, Molinari moves language the way someone moves the clear water of a river with his hand—, only the exquisitely delicate music of the sentences, only the laments of an absent person wounded by absence.

Indefinite, limitless landscapes. Before them the poet, exiled from the landscape, abandoned by nature, abandoned

---

[*] Italics indicate quotes from Molinari's *Day, Time, Clouds*.

64

by himself: *perhaps nobody is thinking, at this moment, of me / I who remain like an angel in nature. / Limpid and absolute as a horizon without bodies or beings.*

Everything and everyone considers him a stranger. He is that being who belongs to no place: *Visitor and distant body / I am recognized by the voices and the light / of these gardens.*

He is the king of a land which only exists in the shapes traced by nostalgia. *A king (…) Tomorrow I will again be alone…* A king always just failing to reach *that impressive and arid kingdom / in the image of thirst.* It is no accident that he mentions his crown several times: *and the wind cleft the thick shadow of the crown / above my eyes.*

If it were not for thirst and nostalgia, he would perhaps be dead. And in truth, there is something dead in Molinari, something devastated—witness the fact that so many of his poems, profoundly rich in linguistic artifice, emit no signal. And he is not only, in some sense, dead; to be dead is precisely one of his deepest, most abiding desires. Yet this desire, being deep and abiding, occasionally rescues and resuscitates the dead part of him. In this way, his ambition to lock himself up like a casket, to lie inert like an object, transmits a singular energy to his most significant poems: *I would like to guard my heart like an enormous castle, / without eyes, without sound, scent, touch, taste, / a useless period of life. Nothing. Not even the sea!*

A thirst for forgetfulness, a thirst to be returned and restored to that *impressive and arid* kingdom his thirst informs him of. Molinari configures the kingdom of absence, of shadows, of what never came, though attractive, if faint and blurry images. This is due, I think, to the ambiguity with which he accepts the gift of imagination. In the middle of the road, he seems to panic and babble: *My suit is worth more than its shadow, more than that kingdom…* He does not consent, however, to redeem the value of the suit—of material reality—, and thus he swings back and forth, suspended between his hunger for material reality and the other kingdom, that of the imagination, whose riches he half despises.

Entirely coherent in his rejections, Molinari also distances himself from another way of knowing: the way of dreams. For the heroic Nerval, dreams were "a deliciously-scented garment worn by fairies." For Molinari, they are but one more cause for disappointment: *I have seen you in my empty dreams.*

Whence his suffering from the uselessness of suffering: *anguish for no one*, one poem reads. Whence also his sense of untenable identity. Even in the midst of his suffering, he lacks the confidence to say: I suffer. *My skin, taste, the night, / know about me, about absence / endured.* Skin, taste, and night: forms of something or someone who knows more about him than he does. The following line reads: *Time is always tomorrow…* In other words, an absent I cannot coincide with the now, with the present, or with presence. The I of these poems is projected toward the unreal and the faraway, which, as it so happens, he never reaches.

We thus come to recognize one of the poet's most persistent faces: the face of disenchantment—*joylessly destined toward a prolonged and resentful disenchantment.* But what was he looking for? He was looking for *The innermost heart of life!* In the face of the failed encounter, there is nothing left but to seal himself off in inexpressible pain: *I no longer know or want to know anything.* And everything is so unstable and alien that not even the certainty of being a wanderer remains: *I'm not sure, but perhaps I'm going away from something, from everything.*

Nostalgia for Another Space

MOLINARI REPEATEDLY EXPRESSES his nostalgia for *another space*. It is an immaculate space, perfect and untouched by time: *Blind and immobile I sing another space: when the air / was filled with flowers, / and the fields were handsome like my countenance and thoughts.* The *other space* is the repository of all fidelity, while oblivion, in addition to being one of the names for infidelity, is, above all, an emblem of the world here below: *And we talk of beings, / of distant shadows: the insatiable, alien murmur / of oblivion over the earth.*

As I have said, Molinari is unable to make the imagination his place of adventure and risk. Consequently, his glimpses of the *other space* are attenuated by the fear of going too far or of touching the bottom. His feelings and intimations regarding *the other* and his description of the mental landscapes that are composed and decompose in the poet's interior space, rather than producing revelatory and illuminating texts are, for the most part, simply pretexts to create a faded atmosphere in which the real is tossed about like a paper boat on a toy fountain. And this is the reason why, independent of his actual values, Molinari is so pleasing, why he is a poet laureate and is so ardently acclaimed: because he points to the *other space* but keeps his distance; because he presents it as a moderated, inoffensive, sweetly sad version of itself. The truth is that Molinari does not want to know the *other space*; what he wants is to flee from it. Whence his continual references to fatigue. He is tired of his unwelcome solitude, tired of passively enduring vague images, tired of uninterpreted dreams. "An uninterpreted dream is like an unopened letter." And in fact there is much of the "unopened letter" in the spiritual world reflected in Molinari's poems.

Consumed by immanence, the poet declares the uselessness of memories just as he affirmed the emptiness of dreams: *Oh sterile recollections, hardly inexhaustible! Who will find my body in the middle of the field, deafened and full of voices?*

This drive to lie inert is repeated in other poems: *Like Endymion I wish for sleep / —the snapping tongue swells my mouth—, / in the shadow of the cedars, the perennials, / the soul fresh, the sleep untroubled by memory.*

Memory—what connects us with the *other space*—is now a noisy, unsettling bedchamber. Against it, nothing better than the dream of the blessed stone. This terror of internal phantoms drives Molinari's inclination—every year more pronounced—toward empty forms, toward an exhausted baroque that converts his poems into hollow spaces where words, whether sleeping or dead, talk without saying anything, or say nothing, or have nothing to say. To be sure, though, such vacuity is also a way of declaring one's misery.

In the midst of a landscape, Molinari informs us about his person, indicating whether it is stationary, whether it contemplates something, whether it is seated, etc. And he is always a figure who stands apart: *On foot, far away, with nothing to drink, I watch the great rivers...* His refusal to engage is so disdainful that it becomes a pathological incapacity to commune with *the innermost heart of life*. Nonetheless, in certain moments that phenomenon is produced which can only happen in the space of a poem, in which the reader establishes a deep connection with the inability—become poetic language—of the poet to connect. Which is to say: the exiled poet, believing himself the only "stranger on the earth," transforms his wound—his exile—into a gathering place. It is difficult for Molinari to be sincere. This privileged encounter therefore only happens in those few poems which manage to express the almost ungraspable images of nostalgia. But nostalgia for what or for whom? For a vagrant paradise, no sooner sensed than lost; for bygone days lived in a dream or another life; in sum, for *another space*.

Days, where are you; ancient blood, call filled with flowers! / (They will not wake up and will never come back, / and will never know about me, just as I know nothing of anyone, / or anything, to the point of loneliest blindness.)

These days and this space are the paradise he is always losing anew *(Oh Eden ever stumbled on)*, his time and place of perfect love *(Where no one can ever take away / the scent of a mouth, / still clinging to my lips)*, and ultimately, the ground where he longs to lie inert until the end of eternity. But in the middle of these diluted aspirations—at no moment do they become religious, in spite of the mention of God—he regrets his failure to reach immediate reality: *I would like to draw happiness from myself; to open my eyes so wide they hurt, / and to stare, to stare at the horizon beyond the void of nostalgia…* And since this is impossible, he yearns to be someone else: *There is a great desire in my throat / —nostalgia or the wind— / a cry that has hardened: to be another being.* And since this also proves impossible, he returns to his image of lying down on the sheltering earth, observed and remembered by nature. From there, in a poem in which he claims to be dead, he expectantly recalls the life that breathes in the trees, the future custodians of his sojourn in the world: *Yet even still they are living, the trees / I saw beneath the tall heavens of the plains.* In effect, if the trees are alive and he is either dead or a shadow, why shouldn't the only survivors be called on to commemorate him…? *perhaps some of them will feel my shadow press the grass / and will remember me, like a long and gentle vanished gale!*

Unlike modern poets, Molinari believes in nature to the point of endowing it with feelings, memory, a sense of sight, desires, and above all, the power to immortalize his image as a wanderer:

*Someday you will think of me, fields, flowers, trees; /
(…) and you will again / see me sitting on riverbanks,
watching the herds of wild horses enter the water / or
how the rushes sway to and fro in the wind and ris-
ing tide.*

Artifices

DESPITE HIS CONSTANT allusions to Argentine landscapes,
Molinari never strays from the Spanish lyric tradition, particularly that of Góngora and other lesser-known Baroque
poets. But Góngora is always precise; nothing could be further from his excesses than absent-mindedness or distrac-
tion. Moreover, by revealing the luxurious, unsuspected face
of the simplest things, even the vulgar ones, he ennobles
them. Not only does Molinari tend to be distracted and im-
precise, he also fails to produce such a transformation. His
sonnets, for example, are like the specters of poem-objects
that, in addition to lacking the energy so notable in works
of the Baroque, considerably dilute and nullify the physical
world they attempt to exalt. Another thing: in the course of
33 years, whatever the design of his poems, Molinari only
has recourse to the rose, the bird, the cloud, the wind, the
carnation, the sky, the day, the river, etc. We can all agree
that poetry is, among other things, artifice, but to attest to
this truth in excess belies a faulty understanding of poetic
artifice. This excess justifies Huidobro's "Enough, sir harp"
and, what is more serious, constitutes a sort of escape from
poetry, even if one believes his work to be at its very center. For the word *poetry* to continue having any meaning,
one must condemn that mixture of conformity, compla-
cency, and inauthenticity entailed by a poem cleverly as-
sembled out of deadest clichés of a given literary tradition
and intended—like a political poem or any other poem that

resorts to formulas and slogans—to flatter the most facile sentiments. In this case, the carnation, the bird, the tree, the wind, the heart, the cloud, etc. are precisely what every frivolous society expects (or rather, deigns to accept) from a poet. At the same time, Spanish America's most preposterous critics habitually consecrate this species of *florid* poem, invariably crediting the author with what has come to be known as "a fine poetic sensibility" ("fine" because it does no one any harm, or any good). As stated above, Molinari's poetry becomes more vacuous with each passing year. To conceal this, he resorts to exclamation points—which might call to mind a vibrating soul—, to reiteration, and to lofty abstract words. An example: *God, my God! Your constricted empty pomp incinerates time...* I hasten to quote a few lines with more life and vitality. They were published in 1534 and their author is Garcilaso: "I also take very seriously the contribution we make to the Castilian language by putting things in it that deserve to be read, because I know not what misfortune has always been ours that almost no one has written anything in our language but that which one could very well excuse..."

A DIFFICULT BALANCE: *ZONA FRANCA*

SURVEYING THE FIRST twenty issues of *Zona Franca*, one can follow the through line—that mercurial line by which we recognize a style—of this journal which, in just a few months, has become one of the best in Latin America.

A biweekly publication in tabloid format, *Zona Franca* stands out for its handsome graphic design. Each issue presents poems, essays, literature reviews (it should be noted that this is one of the very few Spanish-language journals in which the poetry criticism is excellent), notes on the visual arts, theater, film, etc.— especially from Venezuela, but very often from other countries as well. Yet while being, first and foremost, a *journal of literature and ideas*, it is still engaged—by way of its format, its frequent and regular appearance, the issues it tends to discuss, and the rich photographic material it displays—with journalism. I am referring, of course, to that sort of journalism—*luminous and full of spiritual resonance, which one day we will have to rescue from a world characterized by deprivation, arrogance, and the malevolence of the press*—described by Guillermo Sucre (*Zona Franca*, n. 4).

Despite their charming Venezuelanness—or rather, precisely because of it—the editors at *Zona Franca* have succeeded in compiling a truly Latin American journal. From the first issue, they have published texts by writers young and old from across Latin America. What is more, when one is capable of producing a high-quality Latin American journal, one is also endowed with the power to conquer the fear of European literature. That is why *Zona Franca* can feature texts by writers such as Henri Michaux, Eugène Ionesco, Elémire Zolla, René Char, Roger Callois, etc.

The acceptance of contradiction must be the watchword of *Zona Franca*'s creators. Armed with a blazing lucidity, endowed with a healthy aptitude for mediation, they stand face to face with contradictions, taking care not to let themselves be dragged into the zone of tragedy or suicide which seems the natural neighbor to the place of contradiction. It is unnecessary to insist here on the beauty of the tragic, since *Zona Franca*'s editors prefer to situate themselves at the opposite extreme: their guiding principle is specifically to display the other beauty—less visible because less dazzling—of awareness, integration, intervention; in sum, to demonstrate that the path of construction is no less exhilarating than that of destruction. The introductory note on their objectives in the journal's first issue is illuminating in this regard. Below are a few fragments:

> In a world threatened by the possibility of its own mass suicide [...] we constitute a segment of those who call into question [...] that ancestral passion [...] for destroying an enemy without due process of law.

> [...] We believe art that is a form of liberation, that the soul's potential is still intact [...] that lucid doubt is preferable to blind faith.

> [...] This publication's objectives are essentially affirmative. What attracts us more than negation: the creative sense; the propensity for construction; the effort to reconcile different motivations, symbols, human natures.

These words become living and operative on reading *Zona Franca*'s first twenty issues, each of which embodies and elaborates the founders' initial objectives, effectively closing the gap between intention and realization.

In short: an indispensable journal, a gathering place for exceptional texts. Its director is Juan Liscano. Its chief editors are Guillermo Sucre and Luis García Morales. René Char's grand conviction, published in issue 7-8 of *Zona Franca*, could well be addressed to them:

But I know that my peers, amidst innumerable contradictions, possess devastating resources.

RE-READING BRETON'S *NADJA*

> *I left adorable supplicants behind without remorse.*
>> —André Breton,
>> "Surrealism and Painting"

I

A LAUTRÉAMONTIAN LITTLE girl traverses a page of *Nadja* and disappears *with this idea of always plucking the eyes from her dolls to see what's behind them.**

The silent activities of this tiny mutilatrix correspond to Breton's question: *What could be extraordinary about those eyes?*

Eyes like certain terms—*to haunt,* for example—*which say more than they appear to.*

> *Nantes (…), where particular gazes burn with too much fire (I verified this last year, at the time I was driving through Nantes and saw a woman, a worker, I believe, who accompanied a man, and who raised her eyes: I would have had to stop)…*

---

* Italics indicate quotes from Breton's *Nadja.*

Then come the eyes of a disturbed beauty:

Magnificent eyes containing languor, desperation, refinement, cruelty.

And he will address unalterable words to the owner of these magnificently cruel eyes: *I would have had to get closer to her...*

The eyes that yield their spell to Solange close with those that illumined Nantes as soon as Nadja opens her eyes:

I have seen her fern-colored eyes open in the morning upon a world in which the beating of hope's enormous wings is scarcely distinct from the other sounds, which are those of terror, and upon that world I had only seen eyes close.

Like the effigy of the enchanting Gradiva, she advances, light as air. Her style of walking with her head held higher than anyone's is the secret of exiled queens. Still more surprising would be the musical dissonance between Nadja's blonde tresses and the excessive black makeup on her eyes *(I had never seen such eyes)*. Eyes that are transgressive on the street, not in illusory space, even though Solange (Blanche Derval) had never had recourse to makeup. (Solange's eyes, transgressive on stage, not on the street.)

Like her predecessors, the passerby invests the figure of a marvelous, haloed heroine with an air of remoteness. Moreover, Nadja displays *that "declassé" je ne sais quoi that we so admire.* Also worth recalling is the exquisite mark Breton distinguishes in the image of Caroline of Günderode: ... *the moving expression of a promised summer night,* so perhaps it was she, the suicide of the Rhine, who initiated the order of absorbed, nocturnal ladies.

Shadows carved by a black bolt of lightning, these stray beauties find no Hansel and Gretel's cottage in the night, but rather a sister traveler, more somber and more richly endowed with the power of concealment. They embrace and disappear into her like one entering an enchanted cave

(... in this life you'll never find a pleasure greater than the pleasure children derive from the idea of enchanted caves and underground springs).

Just like the fiery blue-eyed canoness, or like Solange, Nadja is a flare sent up between two darknesses. She is the night, the poem that accords only with death.

One fortuitous adventure was enough to make Nadja abandon *this specter of myself condemned to my form in this world*, for Nadja to migrate from herself: *And I abandoned myself being I and being other just like shadows.*

The tempest snatches her and locks her in a house blacker than any imagined by prince or poet from *the coach detained in the night.*

II

And always the only one...
—Nerval

AT THE BEGINNING and the end of *Nadja*, Breton refers to his desire to intersperse the text with photographs of the places, beings, and things that most actively formed a part of him.

An obstinate, mysterious resistance seems to nest in these central images, as if they were impelled by the decision to oppose the project's completion. More surprising is that Breton particularly deplores the impossibility of obtaining the photograph of a figure that not only didn't play a decisive part in his book, but was never even mentioned:

...and above all—for I considered it essential, although it has not elsewhere been referred to in this book—the impossibility of obtaining permission to photograph an adorable waxwork figure in the Grévin Museum, that woman who appears to be fastening her garter in the shadows, and who, in this

immutable posture, is the only statue I know of with eyes, *eyes of provocation.*

There is, perhaps, another statue endowed with such eyes: an oneiric stone statue whose creator, Baudelaire, named *Beauty*. And this Breton specifically rejects in that passage from *Nadja* in which he so extraordinarily defines his vision of the beautiful. It is of course no accident if just before this repudiation he encounters the true woman—not an enchantress, not a sphinx like a *dream of stone*, and not even a vertiginous and fascinating *madwoman*. Simply the beloved.

But invoking another statue does not explain the strange design of inserting an unknown woman's image in *Nadja*. Given that the photographs' function is to complement the text, why the fervent search for the image of a mildly indecent waxen lady?

I can answer with a conjecture (it would be more accurate to say a certainty).

Far from being a stranger, from the beginning of *Nadja*, the immutable lady would have been the object of multiple allusions. And what is more, she would be the sum of the feminine figures that traverse this book, premonitions of the true, the irreplaceable woman that at last appears.

One proof of what has been said is the poet's undifferentiated exaltation before the owner of those eyes he glimpsed in Nantes; before Solange's unsettling presence onstage; before the wide-eyed *sorceress* that is Nadja; and finally, before the illusory wax-hearted creature.

Another proof: the symmetrical repetition of certain details. Not, of course, the obvious details such as the poet's fascination by the eyes of the women in his book. I am referring to privileged details such as the *adorable waxwork figure in the Grévin Museum, that woman who appears to be fastening her garter in the shadows...* This had been preceded, much earlier, by a similar gesture Solange made on stage, a gesture endowed with the same provocative qualities: ... *revealing a magnificent leg, and there, a little above the black garter...*

Later, there is another fleeting scene of dazzling beauty like *the scream, the unforgettable scream* that concludes the play starring Blanche Derval (Solange), or like *the cry, the forever pathetic cry* of the poet asking: *Who goes there?* A perfect scene: near dawn, Solange advances, silent and inexpressive as a doll. Is it really her? *Is it you, Nadja?* There is no reason why it shouldn't be the real ghost of the unreal Solange, or Nadja's reflection, or the figure in the Grévin Museum, seen in some dark mirror.

Solange crosses the stage (...): she walks straight ahead, like an automaton.

III

THE ENTRY FOR October 11, which recounts a brief stroll with Nadja, describes the malaise that sealed that day for Breton, that day suffused with the sense of wasted hours vainly passing. What is more, Nadja *has arrived late and I expect nothing extraordinary from her.*

She who decodes the messages time transmits: Time is a tease. Time is a tease because everything has to happen in its own time. Hoping to invest her sentence with the maximum meaning, Nadja painstakingly repeats it.

Her sentence on time is neither exceptional nor particularly memorable, but it carries significant weight because it addresses one of the keys to Breton and Nadja's labyrinthine adventure...

Time is a tease. Time is a tease because everything has to happen in its own time.

What exactly didn't come (or didn't happen) when it should have come (or happened)?

The encounter between Nadja and Breton. An encounter which didn't take place because Nadja arrived too late. *Nadja has arrived late…*, not the day on which Breton records it, but rather when, dazed by her *fern-colored eyes*, he approached her and they recognized each other (she had smiled like someone who *knows*).

It didn't come when its arrival was necessary, but much later. Thus, instead of an exceptional encounter, what took place was a belated reunion.

In the beautiful and disturbing series of observations that precede Nadja's appearance in his life and his book, Breton relates his deepest desire, the desire whose consummation he most ardently longs for. A desire this great loses force on being transcribed. It is then no more than a shade, neither friendly nor hostile: the memory of a desire.

I have always hoped, beyond belief, to meet a beautiful naked woman in the woods at night, or rather, since a desire once expressed means nothing, I regret, beyond belief, not having met her. Imagining such an encounter is, after all, not to be dismissed as delusion: it could happen. It seems to me that if everything could have stopped short—ah! I would never have found myself writing what I now write. I adore this situation, which of all situations is the one where I would most likely have lost all presence of mind. *I would probably not even have thought of running away. (Anyone who laughs at this last sentence is a pig.)*

It is true that such an encounter could have (and should have) occurred. Yet the opposite is also true: "Dream of her; she will give no other answer."

If one night, by some amazing chance, he had met the naked beauty in the woods (if he had crossed over from desire to reality), Breton would not find himself writing *Nadja*.

The condition of the poet likely brings him, among other things, to adopt the role of a phantom (Breton refers to this in the prelude to his tale). One of the *forced labors* of this phantom might consist of endlessly circling the perimeter of a forest he never manages to enter, as if the forest were a forbidden place.

At the end of the second quatrain her eyes grow moist and fill with visions of a forest. She sees the poet passing near this forest as though she could follow him at a distance.

—*No, he's skirting the forest. He cannot enter, he does not enter.*

Nadja, seated at a café table with Breton, is completely absorbed in a poem by Alfred Jarry, a poem about someone (a poet) who can do nothing but circle around a forest. Suddenly, the spellbound reader slams the book shut:

—*Oh! That is death!*

It is possible that anyone who finds herself facing Breton could be the naked vagrant in the forest of his old desire. Nadja seems to know that the nighttime forest is the place of encounter. She also knows that a transparent understanding, that is to say an understanding based exclusively on love, would no longer be possible between them. Another bond would unite them, no doubt lovely, but inferior to any desire "beyond belief." Perhaps it might be a bond forged by games of back-and-forth: a luminous and illicit movement like that of all true love, and an opposing movement that would force a leap to one's death. *Can't you see what's been happening in the trees? The blue and the wind, the blue wind. (…) And there was a voice saying: "You're going to die, you're going to die." I didn't want to die, but I felt so dizzy…*

It is now too late. Even if the poet manages to enter the forest and find the woman he longed for before, he would not lose his presence of mind and he would even be able to run away. But what is Breton doing in this book if not running away? He runs from Nadja, of course, and he has plenty of reasons to do so, beginning with the first one, Nadja's madness.

Nadja's delay thus signifies an excessively precious sacrifice to the ministry of *trop tard*.

One night, the two friends take the train; when, at the spur of the moment, the poet suggests they get off *at Le Vésinet*, Nadja agrees and suggests *they take a little walk in the woods*.

—No, he's skirting the forest. He cannot enter, he does not enter.

Everything becomes a sign that they arrived at the wrong time. It is too late. *At Le Vésinet, all the lights are out and not a single door will open. The prospect of wandering through the woods is no longer so appealing.*

Nadja's suggestion has been overruled by darkened windows and locked doors, by the term impossible. The conjunction of chance and an irremediable protest by misfortune. For the two nocturnal travelers of Le Vésinet, only one possibility remains, pristine and ironic: returning from nowhere in order to arrive nowhere.

At the end of this marvelous and impossible alliance, Breton wonders about the true Nadja. He has not forgotten the woman who told painful tales of dead and mercenary loves, but he directs the full force of his devotion to the other Nadja, the perfect contrary of *the one who* fell, *at times...*

Breton's commentary on *his* Nadja restores the young woman's dazzling cachet and consummate grandeur. She is the mediator, the intercessor, the *ever-inspired and inspiring creature*; she is a superior instrument of vision and, simultaneously, the apprentice of thugs who chose the streets as a place of instruction and a way of knowing.

And it is this Nadja who told Breton about a simple yet touching stroll. Nadja's narrative affirms, once again, her membership in an exceptionally fine breed of humanity that has no place in this world. More than a stroll, it describes the very essence of wandering, *even though it's night*, through the Forest of Fontainebleau, accompanied by a volatile archaeologist, *in search of who knows what stone remnants.*

Stone and its inexorable representations, the word *remnant*, and, finally, the archaeologist's participation—together, these comprise an ill-starred ceremony at whose heart is the reiterated echo *trop tard*, a kind of exalted *never more*—apt adagio to this woodland song for the wide-eyed girl.

ANDRÉ PIEYRE DE MANDIARGUES'S
THE MOTORCYCLE

THE PLOT OF *The Motorcycle* can be quickly summarized: one morning, Rebecca Nul has a dream that compels her to straddle her powerful motorcycle and hightail it from her husband to her distant lover. Hours later, Rebecca meets death invested with the features of Dionysus. Death and her lover are thus fused in a single, terminal image.

The Motorcycle is made up of erotic rituals which are, simultaneously, pictorial and theatrical scenes that embody a "spatial poetry with the power to create concrete images." Nonetheless, these ceremonies and their exacting rites constitute a novel and, what is more, a novel in which one glimpses the fullness of perfection.

Amid this theatrical tension, the novel's infrequent dialogue emerges—dialogue which offers a plurality of meanings and appears to rest on a false bottom. Consequently, none of the figures in *The Motorcycle* bear the temperamental stamp that would liken them to "characters" in that species of unambiguous suspense drama known as "psychological" theater.

The structure of *The Motorcycle* allows the action to unfold by means of a voice that is constantly shifting between tenses in the form of evocations, present impressions, and future fantasies. It is a judiciously orchestrated counterpoint that testifies to the presence of an ordering vision, one that has released the erotic reveries of girlhood from the slagheap left by Molly Bloom's verbal eruption. The reader of *The Motorcycle* follows the story of an irredeemably fatal journey. By contrast, the central figure who undertakes that journey is unaware of forming part of a drama or even that a drama is occurring.

Inseparable from the trivial details that conjure it up, the concept of fatality derived from Greek tragedy pervades this book. It is no exaggeration—though it might at first appear that way—to invoke such an eminent conception of the tragic. Specifically, in this novel, fatality is drawn to an object corresponding to a rather mundane image: a motorcycle (the coveted Harley Davidson).

Joy, which is constant throughout this book of sex and death, derives from its central theme, namely the consummation (integral to tragedy and death) of sexual desire. Another cause of exultation derives from the ubiquitous vision of death. Because of this vision, lived time takes the place of measured time—the necessary precondition for gaining access to privileged moments. The aspiration to live in poetry is, as is well known, inherent in all of André Pieyre de Mandiargues's work.

Everything in *The Motorcycle* lines up. But it is definitely not a matter of counting up the appearances of certain grave and luminous ideas such as the primitive identity between lust and death. It is more important to underscore that in this novel which narrates a journey, Mandiargues refuses to provide—or even permit—any form of respite other than his equally delicate and savage humor.

A difficult coherence governs this book whose rhythm follows the motorcycle's advance, modulated by the protagonist's evocations of erotic tableaux. But in truth, the novel's rhythm is a direct allusion to the blind motions of the sex act. It suffices to consider the sort of—for lack of a better word—"mechano-eroticism" that exists between the motorcycle and Rebecca's *black bull* or *black slave*, the Harley Davidson; it also suffices to examine the plenitude and abandon of the sex scenes Rebecca and Daniel compose and decompose, and ultimately, to contemplate the final scene, the moment in which the girl, dying brutally, senses that it is not death but her lover who is growing inside her.

There is no one and nothing in this book that cannot become an erotic figure or position. This is so utterly and visibly the case that it is unnecessary to highlight. However, I do want to emphasize the disturbing fact that the garment Rebecca wears—and which forces people to mistake her for an adolescent boy—is a one-piece black leather suit. This detail (which is not a detail but an emblem) is impossible to misinterpret, regardless of any special knowledge of fetish garb: black leather refers to those sexual relations governed by dominance and submission or, more precisely, the sadomasochistic master-slave dialectic. None of this would matter were it not for Rebecca's genuine and absolute submission to her lover—scandalous because it is entirely voluntary and sustained with the greatest of happiness, much like the submission of the Marquise of O, the heroine of that lovely book by the improbable Pauline Réage.

Far from being psychological, the ideas in Mandiargues are largely aesthetic, formal elements. Completely unconcerned with motivations, he continuously refers to a single object which is more than an object: desire. In no instance does he allude to feelings of another kind, not even love. There is only desire.

The writing of André Pieyre de Mandiargues possesses a luminous density, inseparable from the concept of poetry.

Moreover, this wise, beautiful creature, and this syntax like a ritual dance, are aids to the imagination—they *transport* it in the literal sense of the word. Nor is it any wonder that this should be the case, for, as Octavio Paz has written, *Mandiargues's universe is a magic place, built of oppositions and correspondences.*

Mandiargues is always concrete, though he is doubly so when dealing with situations that emerge from our inner shadows. His distant, charming tone does not conceal his admirable disdain for hypocrisy.

Narrated in a tenuous third person singular, *The Motorcycle* presents a number of subtle symmetries and linkages that allow for the innocent and equal cohabitation of the three grammatical tenses, as well as for the disappearance of the boundaries that usually separate them.

In this book where faith in random chance is unconditional, nothing is left to chance. The plot is so carefully circumscribed it can seem like an algebraic delirium.

These details, and many others I haven't mentioned, indicate Mandiargues's passion for accuracy, the passion of a writer who effects the transfer of images from the realm of inner shadow to that of gleaming presence with a precision that defies both accident and chance. Rather than a facile interpretation based on psychology, history, sociology, etc., he prefers the kind of patient description that ensures the integrity of his visions as well as those facts he legitimately invents. Such presence of mind in directing his visionary force testifies to an intense need for poetic truth. In effect, perfection, in Mandiargues, must correspond with freedom.

The concept of order is visible even in Rebecca's irrepressible erotic evocations. Being ever at the breaking point (she is all desire) demands a superior state of clarity; only by constant vigilance can she avoid becoming a puppet in the hands of fate. In the brief calm granted by the dawn—undoubtedly her last—she attempts to outrun the many emblems of death that meet her on the road. Not only does she refuse to give over to thoughts of unthinkable death, she devotes herself to contemplating, one by one, the figures of her impassioned mental scenes: positions, erotic scenarios and tableaux for two actors, Daniel and herself. Few pages are more memorable in this respect than that privileged moment in the *Bath of roses*, the description of which constitutes an excellent poem. But the description of transcendent moments can also take its cue from relatively trivial events. Thus, for example, halfway through her journey, Rebecca drinks a few glasses of kirsch and is suddenly carried away by the brandy's aroma, a mysterious intercessor that fills her with the song of what had been oblivion. The intense communion that emerges between the motorcyclist and her recovered memories vivifies a world that, moments before, was a profusion of meaningless creatures and things. Those instants, images, and conjured gestures derive from a complex linguistic construction. It is for this reason that I have so frequently invoked the word *order*, which in Mandiargues clearly does not indicate the everyday action of putting things in their appropriate place but refers, rather, to the artist's mental drama of organizing living thought. At the same time, it bears repeating that certain positions, tableaux, and erotic configurations would seem to answer Antonin Artaud's demand for *a spatial poetry with the power to create concrete images*. In their hallucinatory, immeasurable duration, those figures and tableaux, whose rhythm recalls the sound of rain striking the ground, halt the flow of the narration. And this is how the massive allusive power of language can be concentrated, for instance, in the portrait of a beautiful girl who dies.

As previously stated, *The Motorcycle*'s narrator is a blurry third person singular who purposely vanishes, much like the director of a play during the performance.

The reference to theater is not arbitrary: the dominion exercised by that which is foreseen, either by chance or by fate, is one of the essential themes of this book. It is what raises the protagonist to the level of tragedy. In the vertigo of speed as she approaches her death, this motorcycle Amazon becomes an ecstatic creature. Rebecca believes she directs her own destiny. But her path is linked with the theater, where every movement has already been determined by the creator's ordering vision. One might say that the underlying principle of *The Motorcycle* is the impossible refutation or the attempt to abolish chance, or, inversely, as in the theater, the possibility of controlling it. In this respect, Mandiargues displays a dual concern: on the one hand, he actively embraces the marvelous idea (inseparable from the rituals of living) of *objective chance*. On the other hand, however, he identifies chance with death. And, of course, this second meaning is more complicated than it may appear.

In *The Motorcycle*, death (or random, unforeseen eclipse) exemplifies the absolute meaning of eroticism. Death and lust are the foundations of this novel, and Mandiargues directs its course with acute objectivity. By emphasizing the enticements of desire alongside the threat of death with such meticulous detachment, he creates a truly merciless liturgy.

NOTE ON JULIO CORTÁZAR'S
"THE OTHER HEAVEN"

Child, certain skies have sharpened my sight...
—Rimbaud

IN "THE OTHER Heaven," a single character confronts the discontinuities of time and space. From this circumstance, two themes emerge: the double, and the man bound to an imaginary exile which, by turning into a hybrid space, determines the wanderer's ultimate banishment to a third and very real exile.

"The Other Heaven" is comprised of two interlocking stories whose central character is the *I* that relates them. The probability (even the certainty) that one of the stories consists entirely of situations imagined by the narrator-protagonist does not compromise its literary autonomy.

The protagonist alternately resides beneath two different heavens: the one first hovers over a Buenos Aires shaken by the aftermath of the Second World War; the other is the artificial sky of nineteenth-century Paris' famed arcades.

In a world whose boundaries have disappeared, where the "I Am" is abused, it becomes "as simple as a musical phrase" to gallivant from one era to another, or from one country to the next. But when the transfer occurs in the middle of a phrase, that phrase takes on the function of a revolving stage. This gives rise to an extended syntax that links together numerous and varied sentences within a single passage: moving grammatical spaces in which the narrator's present time and place coexist with his adventures as a "mental traveler" in Paris or Buenos Aires, his happiness or disappointment on arriving or coming back, descriptions of people, places, his own feelings, and even his first impressions. The narrative schema follows the distinctive pattern of a labyrinth.

"The Other Heaven" consists of two parts, each governed by an epigraph from *Les chants de Maldoror*. The context of the first one alludes to depersonalization, to the fear of losing one's memory or identity, to the double. Cortázar transcribes Lautréamont's "dreadful accusation" of the shadowy intruder in his room: *Those eyes don't belong to you... Where did you take them from?**

(LAUTRÉAMONT DIRECTS HIS inadjectivable violence against the intruder. This does not exempt him from having to recognize in her the highest perfection in the field of perversion. No one but the shadow deserves the consummate accolade, "the palm of evil." Lautréamont exhibits his equivocal desire to kiss the vanquisher's feet, but were he in fact to prostrate himself before her, nothing but a transparent plume of steam would convey the rejection. He quickly finds that it is the other (or the shadow), not himself, who is the ironist.

In the search—a full-blown hunt—for the shadow body, the other pretends to collaborate with the poet, the better to betray him. Scarcely has he demanded, via a signal, that the shadow stay put than it imitates his gesture. This is

---

* Italics indicate quotes from Cortázar's "The Other Heaven."

how he discovers the shadow's secret and, in consequence, the necessity of breaking the mirror in his garret. He concludes that it isn't the first time "I've found myself faced with the non-recognition of my own reflection.")

Recalling the Galería Güemes of his teenage years, the narrator describes an experience that combines an interest in mint candy with flat-rate trysts and newspapers advertising *evening editions with full-page crime spreads*. But the diverse correspondences he includes in his narration are not sufficient to expose the spellbinding power and cachet which the tender passerby ascribed to the arcades. One is thus led to think of more hidden forces: the arcades become sites which embody the impossible. At least this is how they would appear to the teenage lover of places where it is always night— a contrived and illusory night, but one in which *the stupidity of the day and the sun outside* are unknown. And insofar as the impossible is synonymous with the forbidden, the Galería Güemes is revealed as the prohibited place one simultaneously desires and fears to enter.

Years later, the mysterious adolescent still breathes inside an adult now employed as a stockbroker. His attraction to arcades has intensified and he chooses as his favorite place the Galerie Vivienne, a little world of innocent beauty found in the Paris of the nineteenth century. There he meets the charming prostitute Josiane. It matters little how the relocation occurs; the essential thing is that an impossible desire has been elevated to an autonomous plane on which one operates with miraculous ease. As for Josiane, the probability that she is a phantom emanating from a visionary does not impede her being perceived as more alive, more lovable, and more compelling than the real-life Irma.

The stockbroker's double life presents several radical and irresolvable differences. His deepest desires call for an *elsewhere*, whereas here he is subject to the claims of his mother and his girlfriend, simply named Irma. To make matters worse, the conflict is compounded by the dreamer's fear of wholly succumbing to his innermost urge. It is true that this urge or call involves idle fantasies, by contrast with the very real sense of loneliness and exile experienced by those who demand of the imaginary what poets demand of language, namely that it be their authentic homeland. On the other hand, the journey to the *port of repose* entails extreme hardships. Suffice it to mention the splitting of the self and the certainty (and terror) of being two, or the fear of losing one's identity and the despair that results from projecting fabulous psychic creatures into the real world. Nevertheless, the dreamer steps inside internal night or, what amounts to the same thing, he leaves himself, frees himself from his own character, and is lost in the encounter.

In *the secret homeland*, there is someone strange and alien who stands out for being present and absent at the same time. He is the murderer known as Laurent (when something—including nothingness—has a name, it seems less hostile), whose singularity consists in transforming "women of pleasure" into women of death. So completely does *everything appear to be ordered around that neighborhood terror* that even language ends up becoming impoverished: whatever *loose phrases* people say *are instantly applied to Laurent*. The language of terror spreads to the other side of the narrative and soon the stockbroker's colleagues and clients speak only of Laurent. This fugitive, untimely betrayal of the principle of symmetry (by which here and there are entirely separate) attests to a frighteningly relativistic sense of time and space.

The *secret homeland* is divided into *the marvelous* (hourless time, time with Josiane, angels of the little *galerie*…) and *the sinister* (snowfall and the cold seem to be in solidarity with the killer and the outdoors becomes an ominous allegory). The stockbroker cannot but feel thankful for *the sinister* because, for him, it signifies the pleasure of limitless time in the company of Josiane.

Who is Laurent?

A literary trope as old as it is fascinating links the theater with life. "The Human Comedy" and "The Great Theatre of the World" are but two of the titles which confirm that "life is a farce we all must act." An equally ancient and beautiful plot affirms that no one can choose the role he will have to play. Thus, the role of death must have been assigned to Laurent. And it is no accident if Cortázar endows him with the gift of concealment.

Since bygone times, death has been perceived as the concealed that conceals. As for the act of killing, it entails a fusion with death which, in turn, implies an identification with the unknown, ever-lurking assassin. Like death, Laurent operates in shadow, and no one understands why or how or for what reason he bursts forth, inexplicably acts, and disappears. Like the dead in regard to death, only Laurent's victims can know his full presence.

How did Laurent get to the *other heaven*? It is worth recalling certain old refrains that used to clang in the air of the Galería Güemes: *they were hawking the late editions with full-page crime spreads*. A sort of binary substance composed of Eros and death thus constitutes the original clay from which Laurent was formed.

This unseen golem has one exclusive and invariable faculty: finishing off prostitutes—a faculty intimately connected to the epigraph from Lautréamont and, even more so, to the context from which it is taken. It can be deduced from this that Laurent came to possess his blue eyes by removing them from some victim of his grim, shadowy hands. But here it should be remembered that Lautréamont quarreled with a shadow that turned out to be his own, such that

Laurent is he, Lautréamont. Add to this the coincidence that the first syllable of the invented name Laurent is the same as that of the pseudonym Lautréamont. And it just so happens that the central figure in the *arcade district* is a South American teenager easily identified as Isidore Ducasse, the Count of Lautréamont.

Lautréamont regularly visits the café favored by the story's happy lovers. This is where the tensest and most intense scene occurs, though it is also so simple that it seems odd to have to assign it such apprehensive, solemn terms.

The scene is as follows: one night, the narrator comes to the beloved café. The South American appears soon after. *I* resolves to get closer and talk with him. Something stops him, however, imposing itself during the brief instant that corresponding to the passage from the desire to its realization, and *now I am no more than one of the many people who wonder why, at a given moment, they didn't do what they had intended to.* He claims to have forgotten *what it felt like to give up my impulse* while still recalling that the forgotten feeling was like transgression, like entering *hostile territory.*

Certainly, such dread before the emissary and keeper of the forbidden appears crystal clear and quite understandable. But perhaps we should reconsider one conflict that is never resolved: the stockbroker manages to exempt himself from an unimaginably terrifying confrontation with madness and death; at the same time, though, he realizes that he thereby lost the chance to save himself from God-knows-what.

And I nevertheless feel I've done wrong, that I was on the verge of an act which could have saved me.

My sense is that in the depths of his soul he realizes that this meeting with the other would have freed him. Among other things, he would have managed to move beyond that species of introductory poetry course that would become his revolving stage and, if it transports him to the *other heaven*, also returns him to Buenos Aires, which amounts to the indefinite endurance of ambiguity.

The protagonist claims he did not dare to take the definitive step. To which I would add my own surmise: it is irrelevant whether or not he could bring himself to take the definitive step because someone else took it for him. This someone else is his double: a poet who lost his way in search of the things that fundamentally concern us.

In this way, the Montevidean gives rise to a *doppelgänger*, many years after his death, though quite close to his native country. What remain are Laurent's adventures as a double raised to the second power—a sort of "third man" that emerges from two characters who are one and the same.

In the second part of the tale, the *secret homeland* has been deprived of its former power to enchant and protect. Transformed into the stomping grounds of crime and war ("pseudonyms for reality"), *I* attempts to cope with this tremendous loss. To no longer have a *place of rest*, however illusory. Exiled in a state of intolerable purity. One can die of such things: *one dies of less.*

Not far from the second epigraph, the Count of Lautréamont poses a very fitting question for our desolate traveler: *Why not rather consider as an abnormal fact the ability he has shown until now to feel exempt from anxiety and, so to speak, happy?*

On his final trip to the *other heaven*, he learns that Laurent has been arrested; he is also informed of the South American's death. The double news inspires this parallelism: *the two deaths* (…) *struck me as symmetrical, the South American's and Laurent's.* This constitutes a symmetrical, definitive attack on his happiness. To corroborate it, he marries his girlfriend.

Irma's husband rejects the mere idea of never going *there* again, but his resolute denial of this possibility only confirms it. What proves much richer in meaning is his conviction of having suffered the most irremediable loss at the hands of the South American, *as if he had murdered Laurent and myself with his own death.* The end of this sentence reminds me of a detail in *Nadja*: André Breton alludes to the death of the delightful Montevidean while avoiding the verb *to die*—so easy, so intransitive. Instead, he refers to his *complete disappearance.* And further: *I find something supernatural in the circumstance of such a total human erasure.*

Lautréamont dead, the stockbroker does not (and will never) go back to the *other heaven.* As the proverb says: *When the man dies, so does his shadow.*

In "The Other Heaven," Julio Cortázar has deliberately and fatally configured a quarrel symmetrical to the one Maldoror sustains with his own shadow. But "The Other Heaven" is, first and foremost, a place of encounter with 'convulsive beauty' and a perfection that is more than a little terrifying. It is heartening to know that we will never discover the identity of *the other* who hounds the secret personal pronoun, telling a tale where that which is most real is philosophical drama.

THE INCARNATE WORD

> *I blame the men of this age for causing me to be*
> *born by the most infamous magical maneuvers*
> *into a world I wanted no part of, and for trying*
> *by similar magical maneuvers to prevent me from*
> *making a hole in this world in order to leave it.*
> *I need poetry to live, and I want to see it around*
> *me. And I do not accept the fact that the poet who*
> *I am was committed to an insane asylum because*
> *he wanted to realize his poetry in its natural state.*
> —Antonin Artaud, *Letters from Rodez*

THAT ASSERTION OF Hölderlin's, that "poetry is a dangerous game," has its real equivalent in several famous sacrifices: the suffering of Baudelaire, the suicide of Nerval, the premature silence of Rimbaud, the mysterious and ephemeral presence of Lautréamont, the life and work of Artaud...

These poets, and a few others, are linked by having annulled—or having tried to annul—the distance society imposes between poetry and life.

Artaud still hasn't entered university curricula, as is the case with Baudelaire. So it's appropriate, in this little note, to appeal to a mediator the caliber of André Gide, whose testimony gives a good account of the convulsive genius of Artaud and his work. Gide wrote this text after that memorable evening, January 13, 1947, at the Vieux Colombier, where Artaud—recently released from the asylum at Rodez—tried to explain himself with—but it couldn't be "with," rather "before"—the others. This is the testimony of André Gide:

> In the back of the auditorium—that dear old auditorium of the Vieux Colombier that could hold about 300 people—there were half a dozen pranksters who had come to the event looking to have a laugh. Oh! I still think their insults could have gotten them locked up by Artaud's fervent friends, scattered throughout the auditorium. But no: after one very timid attempt at a ruckus there was no need to intervene…We were present at an astonishing spectacle: Artaud triumphed, deflecting the mockery and insolent jeers; he dominated…
>
> I had known Artaud for a long time, both his anguish and his genius. Never before had he seemed more admirable to me. Nothing remained of his material being but expression. His tall, gangly silhouette, his face consumed by an internal flame, his hands flailing like a drowning man's, now stretched toward some unreachable aid, now twisted in agony, but most often clasped tightly over his face, alternately hiding and revealing it—everything in him displayed the horror of human misery, a damnation without appeal, with no possible escape but a furious lyricism which only reached the public in bursts of obscenity, imprecations, and blasphemy. Here, without a doubt, we encountered the astonishing actor this artist could turn himself into; but it was his own person he offered to the public in a kind of shameless farce that disclosed a total authenticity. Reason fled in defeat, not only his own but that of the entire audience, all of us, spectators at that hideous drama, reduced to the roles of malevolent stage extras, jackasses, and yokels. Oh, no! No one in the audience wanted to laugh anymore;

and what's more, Artaud extinguished our desire to laugh for a long time to come. He had forced us into his tragic game of revolt against everything that we accepted but that he, who was purer than we, permanently refused:

> We haven't been born yet.
>
> We aren't in the world yet.
>
> There isn't any world yet.
>
> Things aren't made yet.
>
> The reason for being hasn't been found yet...

At the end of that memorable event, the public was speechless. What could they have said? They had just seen a miserable man, brutally beaten by a god, as if on the threshold of a deep cavern, the secret den of the Sybil where nothing profane is tolerated, or rather, they had seen, as if on a poetic Mount Carmel, the *vates* stripped naked, offered up to the storm, to birds of prey, at once victim and priest... And we felt ashamed to take up our places again in a world where comfort consists of compromise.

A WRITER WHO signs himself L'Alchimiste, after tracing a convincing parallel between Arthur Rimbaud and Antonin Artaud, discerns in their works a "white period" and a "black period," separated in Rimbaud by the "Letter of a Seer" and in Artaud by "The New Revelations of Being" (1937).

What is most astonishing about Artaud's "white period" is his extraordinary need for incarnation, while in the "black period" there is a perfect crystallization of that need.

The writings of the "white period," be they literary, cinematic, or theatrical, all attest to that prodigious thirst to liberate and restore to the living body that which remains imprisoned by words.

> *I entered the world of literature writing books in order to say that I could write absolutely nothing; when*

> *I had something to say or write, thought was what abandoned me the most. I never had ideas, and two or three little books of sixty pages each revolve around this deep, inveterate, endemic absence of all ideas. They are* The Umbilicus of Limbo *and* Nerve Meter.*

It is particularly in *Nerve Meter* that Artaud describes the narcotically confused state (and it is painfully ironic to be unable to stop admiring the magnificent "poetry" of this book) of his language in relation to thought. His central wound is internal paralysis and the hideous privations that result from it: the inability to feel the rhythm of his own thought (in its place lies something that has always been shattered) and the inability to feel that human language is alive: *All the terms I choose to think with are for me TERMS in the proper sense of the word, absolute terminations...*

There is a word Artaud repeats throughout his writings: *effectiveness.* It is closely related to his need for *metaphysics in action,* and as used by Artaud it means that art—or culture in general—must be effective in the same way that our respiratory system is effective:

> *I don't believe the most urgent task is to defend a culture whose existence never freed a man from concerns about living a better life or going hungry, but rather to extract from this so-called culture ideas whose vital force is the same as that of hunger.*

And if you ask what that consists of, at the level of poetry, that effectiveness Artaud desired as nobody else and found as nobody else, this statement from Marcel Granet (*Chinese Thought*) may be a useful response:

> To know the name, to say the word, is to possess the being or create the thing. Every beast is tamed by the man who knows how to name it... I have tigers for soldiers if I call them: "tigers!"

---

* Quotations from Artaud appear in italics.

The main works of the "black period" are: *A Journey to the Land of the Tarahumaras; Van Gogh: The Man Suicided by Society; Letters from Rodez; Artaud the Mômo; Indian Culture and Here Lies;* and *To Have Done with the Judgment of God.*

They are indefinable works. But to explain why something is indefinable may be a way—perhaps the noblest way—of defining it. This is what Arthur Adamov does in an excellent article in which he lays out the impossibilities—which I sum up here—of defining Artaud's work:

Artaud's poetry has almost nothing in common with poetry that has been classified and defined.

The life and death of Artaud are inseparable from his work "to a degree that is unique in the history of literature."

The poems of his last period are a "kind of phonetic miracle that ceaselessly renews itself."

One cannot study Artaud's thought as if it had to do with thinking since Artaud did not forge himself by thinking.

MANY POETS REBELLED against reason in order to replace it with a poetic discourse that belongs exclusively to Poetry. But Artaud is far from them. His language has nothing poetic about it even though a more effective language doesn't exist.

Given that his work rejects both aesthetic and dialectical judgments, *the only key* that can provide a reference point is the effect it produces. But this is almost impossible to speak of since the effect is the equivalent of a physical blow. (If one asks where such force comes from, the answer is, from the utmost physical and moral suffering. The drama of Artaud is that of us all, but his defiance and his suffering are of an unparalleled intensity.) Reading the late Artaud in translation is like looking at reproductions of Van Gogh's paintings. And this, among many other causes, is due to the corporeality of the language, to the respiratory stamp of the poet, to his absolute lack of ambiguity.

YES, THE WORD was made flesh. And also, and above all in Artaud, the body was made word. Why then his old lament over his separation from words? Just as Van Gogh restores to nature its forgotten nobility, and to manmade things their maximum dignity, thanks to those sunflowers, those old shoes, that chair, those ravens…so too, with identical purity and identical intensity, the word of Artaud, that is to say Artaud himself, rescues "humanity's abhorrent misery" by incarnating it. Artaud, like Van Gogh, and very few others, leaves us works whose primary difficulty is rooted in the place—inaccessible to almost everyone—where they were made. Any approach to them can only be real if it takes the terrifying roads of purity, lucidity, suffering, patience…

> …returning to Antonin Artaud after his ten years of misery, to begin to glimpse what he meant, what this sign cast among us means, perhaps the last one worth deciphering…

MICHAUX'S *PASSAGES*

HENRI MICHAUX'S MOST recent book is a reissue, expanded and corrected, of *Passages*. It consists of 20 texts we could call *essays* even though they partake of the highest poetry. Michaux summons so many aspects of himself in *Passages* that one could speak separately of Michaux the painter, the musician, the lover, the traveler, the cold, patient observer, the disproportionate exorcist, etc., etc. But even if we consent to making these distinctions, they must be distinguished in greater depth. For instance, if we think of Michaux the humorist (humor is one of his fundamental traits), we discover that it is not a humor that can be conclusively defined. Sometimes he appears to possess a delicious, extremely direct humor (one example would be the brutal and amusing diatribe he inflicts on swans). But at other times his laughter is closer to that of his comrade Lautréamont. We hear it in this book when, with the patience of an entomologist, he amasses examples that testify to the horror and insanity that belong to our age and, in particular, to western man.

In terms of the themes in *Passages*, they are so many and so varied that simply enumerating them might bring to mind a surrealist poem: the song of the sirens; the case of the two little Indian girls raised by a she-wolf; a new model of the sacred host; horses getting high; the text of a youth from the year 4,000 (of our common era); the cruelty of Mistral winds; poetry and traveling; curses; space and painting; Paul Klee's lines; Michaux's own experiences with drawing and painting as well as his experiences—or experiments—as a composer; flies; the fairies of the Rhine; the origin of his famous character "Plume;" bees; tigresses; life before birth; etc., etc.

The title of the book, *Passages*, could well be the title of Michaux's entire oeuvre, which is synonymous with searching for a *passage*, opening a breach, forging clarity in darkness. Haven't they said "the poet is the great therapist?" Michaux demonstrates this better than anyone. His insatiable appetite for knowledge is only equaled by his quest for liberation. This is why, in the space of the poem as much as the painting, Michaux fights, yells, pursues, is pursued, groans, reveals, illuminates... His poems aren't only evidence of this century's greatest poetry, they are also exercises in liberation and ways of knowing. And the extraordinary thing is that, being the individual attempts of the man Michaux to exorcize his own sufferings and obsessions, they support and console the reader more than any storehouse of benevolent sentiments about the brotherhood of man.

Michaux reconsiders everything with the eyes of a newcomer. And it is lovely to see that his enormous learning has not overshadowed that gaze from the first day of Creation. This is why it comes as no surprise that so many themes in *Passages* are the object of unexpected considerations, of thoughts that never occurred to anyone else before. The point is that Michaux is not afraid "to see the infinite in a grain of sand" (his courage, in this sense, is the equivalent of Rimbaud's, Dostoyevsky's, or Artaud's).

Personally, I have read and re-read with particular

excitement the chapters in which the poet refers to painting, music, and childhood. What I submit, then, is a brief summary of these re-readings, interspersed with as many excerpts from Michaux himself as possible.

Painting

MICHAUX COMMENTS ON his own painting in various chapters, on painting in general, and on that of Paul Klee. Referring to his own works, Michaux presents them as "passages" leading to a sort of center from which gestures (every gesture) and movements (every movement) emanate. In other words: he wants to return, by way of his drawings and paintings, to the place where our inner self flows in its maximum purity. He wants, in drawing, *to reveal the internal sentence, the sentence without words, a sinuous cord unwinding indefinitely. I wanted to draw the awareness of being and the flowing of time the way you take someone's pulse.**

And painting for Michaux—like writing and music—is a form of liberation, as much a reconquest of primordial health as a way of understanding (understanding man, of course, but on whom does one experiment if not on oneself? There's no one else on hand...): *Undertaking the first lines I felt, to my great amazement, that something which had always been closed had opened in me, and that a great quantity of movement was going to pass through the breach.*

Of Paul Klee's lines, Michaux says that *in a simple little herb garden*, they create the *labyrinth of eternal return.*

And for those who are frightened by the continuous revolutions of contemporary painting, behold that Michaux himself finds them insufficient. What remains to be liberated, he tells us, is the *space* of the painting.

---

* Italics indicate quotes from Michaux's *Passages.*

Music and Silence

MUSICAL SOUNDS CAN destroy the firm borders of things. As a result, something begins to flow and the composer (as well as the listener) *becomes the captain of a RIVER...*

> *Silence is my voice, my shadow, my key...*
>
> [Silence] *unfolds, drinks me, consumes me.*
>
> *The enormous bloodsucking leech goes to sleep inside me.*

Against silence, words. But Michaux mistrusts words too much: blunt weapons, broken instruments. And what's more: signals to lurking hostile forces:

> *Words, words that come to explain, to discuss, to revoke, to justify, rationalize, reify—prose like a jackal.*
>
> *I must never forget: I was suffocated. I was crushed between words.*

Therefore, against silence and against words: a piano. I want to dwell on what Henri Michaux says about the piano because no one has ever said it so perfectly:

> *A companion who does not observe me, assess me, comment, keep records, who neither demands nor compels me to promise him anything.*
>
> *It is all so simple with him.*
>
> *I approach. He is ready.*
>
> *I bring him obsession, tension, oppression:*
>
> *He sings.*
>
> *I bring him a hopeless situation, a vain display of effort, the meanness and failure of everything, precautions carried off by the wind, by fire, by fire, above all by fire:*
>
> *He sings.*

I bring him torrents of blood, the dissonant braying of donkeys, fields, forced labor, poverty, the prisoners of families, things done halfway, halfway love, impulses felt halfway and less than that, skinny cows, hospitals, police interrogations, the agonizing slowness of forgotten villages, bitter survivors, the damaged, those who wander the deranged frozen hillside with me:

He sings.

I carry everything in disarray, not knowing what I bring, who it comes from, who it's for, or who is speaking in the basket of wounds:

He sings.

He sings.

For those who know how to look, everything becomes a search. To approach the piano and let it sing is to approach the piano and let myself sing. But above all, it is to transform the encounter with the piano into a scene of learning: *What I would like is a music that can question, examine, bring me closer to the problem of being.* Michaux does not want to compose like a composer, especially not like a western composer: he wants to make the music of a sparrow, *a somewhat indecisive sparrow, perched on a branch, a sparrow trying to call a man…*

He wants a music that can call for help in the horror, in the not-knowing, a music that can speak of his dispossession, a music like no other's, similar only to himself, a music by which to recognize himself, to speak his name, a music that can mark his place, that expresses his lack of place:

A poor melody, poor like the melody a beggar would need to wordlessly describe his misery, the misery all around him, and everything that answers his misery with misery but does not hear him.

Like a plea for suicide, like a suicide underway, like an eternal return to the only recourse: suicide, melody.

> *A melody of relapses, a melody to buy time, to beguile the serpent while the tireless brow keeps searching, in vain, for its East.*

Music's *miniscule waves* console us *for the intolerable "solid state" of the world, for all the consequences of this state, all its structures...* Time, thanks to music, becomes *something we can savor.*

The Gaze of Childhood

IT IS NOT given to man to know his own kind, nor to know the child he once was: he was a child but he forgot it, he has completely forgotten *the interior atmosphere* of his childhood. The issue, then, is the loss of the memory of the *time of childhood*. Michaux speaks of the child's gaze:

> *The gazes of children, so particular, so rich in unknowing, rich in extension, in emptiness, large through ignorance, like a river that flows (the adult has sold extension for milestones on the road), gazes still unmoored, dense with everything that escapes them, full of what hasn't been deciphered yet. Gazes from the outside...*

In another part of the book, Michaux attributes similar qualities to the faces of little girls, which are as irrecoverable as man's former gaze. The beauty of these faces is due to the fact that, for a very brief time, they are faces *without an "I."* Michaux calls them *faces without a captain*, since no one inhabits them yet, no one directs them...

Meditating on this idea of the irrecoverable, I ask myself: And the memory of Proust? And the taste and the smell of childhood that Proust rescues in a way that seems perfect to us? Michaux denies the possibility of such recuperation:

> *...man was once a child. He remained one for a very long time, but apparently in vain. Something essential,*

an inner atmosphere, the je ne sais quoi that linked ev-
erything together, disappeared, taking with it the en-
tire world of childhood (…) the scent of childhood is
buried deep inside us (…) and cannot be recovered.
The Time of the child, that extraordinary Time, a
physiological Time created by a different explosion, a
different rhythm in the blood and respiration, a differ-
ent rate of healing, is now completely lost to us…

Michaux illustrates this definitive loss with a magnificent example:

At eight years old, Louis XIII makes a drawing simi-
lar to one the son a New Caledonian cannibal makes.
At eight years old, he's the age of humanity, at least
two hundred and fifty thousand years old. A few years
later those years are lost, he isn't more than thirty-one,
he has become an individual, nothing more than a
French king, a morass he will never escape.

ILLICIT DOMAINS

THE EXTREME CONCENTRATION of these stories—some of them only a page and a half long—manifests the design to radically abolish the subservient parts of the tale. By excluding the interventions of empty meaning, everything appears as primary, or more accurately, it *is* primary.

Disobedience to the predetermined formulas of the short story would seem to give rise in the author of *The Mortal Sin* to the wisdom which distinguishes the children in her story "The Inextinguishable Race." They don't accept the imperfect cities of *those people,** the adults; consequently, they build another one, *little and perfect*. The structure of these narratives is no otherwise: little and perfect, as complete as a flower or a stone.

Delicate reserve and a talent for allusion are aspects of a "simple," rigorous writing that cannot disguise its perfection. Here everything is "much clearer" and at the same time, much more dangerous. The danger lies in the fact that the texts incessantly say something more, something else, than what they say. In addition, the everyday world remains recognizable, though strange and transformed: suddenly it

---

* Italics indicate quotes from Ocampo's *The Mortal Sin*.

111

opens up and is *other*, or reveals *the other*, but the transition is entirely imperceptible. Silvina Ocampo's ambiguity corresponds with her ability to transpose a common, harmless fact into another which remains the same, only disturbing. In other words, she shifts the plane of reality without ever having left it. Likewise, she shifts the plane of unreality without ever having left it. Clearly, words like *reality* and *unreality* are entirely inadequate. But in order to suggest certain gestures and movements with greater accuracy, one would have to refer, in this case, to the tenuous bodily script of Japanese dance. Meanwhile, it is worth recalling Sterne: "There are certain looks of such complicated subtlety…"

The practice of making childhood passions visible constitutes the magnetic center of the present collection. Of course, a hasty commentary such as this one cannot lead to the "sacred and illicit domain" of childhood. At the same time, it can scarcely avoid the little beings one encounters there.

In the story "The Mortal Sin" there is a girl, fascinating in her urgency to express forms of debauchery and to participate in primitive festivals where sensual games rhyme harmoniously with her other games. Failing this, she must serve as both officiant and sacrificial victim of her own black masses in which her guileless lover is distinguished: a red mimosa.

The child in "Autobiography of Irene" also befriends a character of similar provenance to the mimosa: *Jazmín*, an imaginary dog. Furthermore, the two girls share *the burning desire to be a saint* or, perhaps, to drown themselves in the velvety waters of a guiltless dream.

But Doll, by contrast with Irene, is a lovable figure due to her wide-open eyes. She knows that the red mimosa and the *missal bound in white* she has invested with aphrodisiac properties are captivating and terrifying because they are signs of the forbidden. The irrepressible desire for and terror of transgression confer a desperate, dazzling prestige on those simple acts executed with identical mastery by a tiny savage and any king's little boy.

In the most beautiful scene, the mimosa is replaced by Chango, *the chief servant, the right-hand man of the house*. The man with the mouth of a viper, the luxuriously-dressed girl who is inseparable from her doll, and the rites of death come together to create an exquisitely violent spectacle. Quiet and inexpressive, Doll consents to become a doll played with by a phantasmal, unctuous character. Simultaneously, in the adult area of the house, a wake is being held. *Someone died, I don't remember who.* The presence of death, gently suggested, is conclusive. On one hand, it is surrounded by ceremonies; it too belongs to the forbidden. On the other hand, the disorder death always creates gives an order to the horror and uncertainty of the ceremonies previous to the forbidden day on which a girl finds a name for her nonexistent guilt. The scene is designated: *ancient performance*. Perhaps it might also be possible to add that the *performance* convenes the *Danses macabres*, possibly because they derive from a continual theme: Death and Lust.

The following detail emerges from the *ancient performance*: Doll, who is inseparable from her doll, is witness to—and possibly a participant in—sensual practices which are exceedingly faithful to *the school of voyeurism*. And when *the right-hand man of the house* asks if she saw and if she liked it, Doll rips out the hair of her doll, which constitutes an answer. ("This man makes his doll laugh." Fargue.) The splendid and erotic simulacrum we call *doll* appears, here, like the *doppelgänger* of Doll performing a splendid erotic simulation.

According to the writer of the prologue, "Icera" and "The Inextinguishable Race" illustrate a topic in fantastic literature that consists of *warping time, and above all, disregarding its quality of irreversibility…*

Indeed, in both "Icera" and "The Inextinguishable Race," the warping of space is conspicuous (the idea of space implies, of course, that of the body itself). In both stories, time takes the form of space or, what amounts to the same thing, time is transformed into space. In the first story, Icera, an unusually tiny little girl, decides to never grow up. Her choice precedes that of Oskar Matzerath (*The Tin Drum*), a historical circumstance mentioned because it was prefigured, in some way, in another story, "The magic pen."

In order to remain exactly as she is, Icera gives herself over to spiritual asceticism. She is aided by her faith and, above all, by her ignorance of the characteristic adult expression, "as far as possible." At the same time, the cautious little one martyrizes her diminutive body with diminutive dresses and shoes, by means of which she chances to invent a growth belt or a childhood belt. The experiment is successful—physically, metaphysically, and morally.

"The Inextinguishable Race" inhabits a miniature city where *everything is perfect and small: the houses, the furniture, the tools, the stores, the gardens.* In spite of these delicious spaces, opacity looms over the story. Perhaps because the children, with their usual responsibility, have taken charge of the adult or lazy class, and they appear overwhelmed. But the adults feel misunderstood and dissatisfied; they therefore have no other option than to misbehave.

The most perfect metamorphosis of space occurs in "The Staircase." This story in the form of Epinal prints proves that seventy years of life can be transmuted into twenty-five steps. On the last step, space and time mutually destroy each other: it is the end of the staircase; it is an old woman's death.

"Icera" and "The Inextinguishable Race" bear witness

to the refutation of adult space. At the opposite extreme are Fernando ("Voice on the Telephone"), Doll ("The Mortal Sin") and Lucio ("The Guests"), confined in houses too big for eyes so fresh. True, those houses possess a secret and threatening beauty that children admire with joy and cruelty when they discover it in children's books. But if a house is that which protects, it is obvious that these children inhabit illusory houses.

The game of theatrical illusion is amplified by the presence of "the third party." To this character, one of the servants, *the fathers and mothers* assign the following role: that of intervening between themselves and the children. He also operates in proximity to poor children, with the difference that they seek him out of their own volition. They thus form equivocal triangles, and it is no coincidence that these "third parties" have feminine and motherly traits (we have seen an example: Chango). The exception to the rule would seem to be Ireneo ("The Arabian") insofar as he excessively confirms it.

The dialectic of abandonment and humor is intrinsic to all of the stories. Accordingly, a mutilated childhood finds its complement in the *vendetta* of childhood. That dreaded word immediately conjures up Fernando ("Voice on the Telephone"), author of the most memorable *vendetta*. He executes it, of course, at one of the birthday parties Silvina Ocampo scrupulously organizes in honor of her "guests." After reading this book, we understand that the calendar is an instrument which records how much time is left before a birthday.

Besides being a four-year-old *nouveau riche*, Fernando is a worshipper of matches, thanks to the "third party" and his mother, who constantly presents him with a problem of causality: *Fernando, if you play with matches, you'll burn down the house*. And Fernando, like all small children and all great scientists, must gauge the dose of truth contained in the problem. The birthday party thus becomes apotheosis or, more modestly, a trauma: Fernando plays with matches and burns down the house. As for *the mothers*, they naturally die by fire.

This tiny pyromaniac is not the only parricide. Rather, there is no child in *The Mortal Sin* who is not one. "Autobiography of Irene" bears witness to an imaginary parricide. On the day of her first communion, Doll enters the church *with the pain of a parricide*. One exception is Luis ("The Arabian"): the only thing he does is abandon his mother for a horse.

Like all children, but a little more so, the ones in this book see and hear what they should not, what they cannot. This is not simply a matter of the classic, lascivious pilfering of scenes and sounds; it involves something more serious: the discovery of their "mortal sin," that is, the reason why *those people* handed them over to the fury of *solitary panic*.

In the stories of Silvina Ocampo, the miserable are "visited by jokes" without any consequent reduction of either humor or affliction.

Two effective examples: "The Velvet Dress" and "The Photographs." The first is a sketch in which a lady is trying on a seamstress' dress. The fitting is interrupted because the client dies inside the dress-turned-prison. That is all, and the silent treason of a dress isn't laughable, or even surprising. But Silvina Ocampo entrusted the handling of the story to one of the seamstress' friends: the delighted, hilarious dwarf of a woman responsible for covering a trivial event taken from the dregs of everyday life with the distinguished mask of a barbaric ritual. The humor, and a delicate horror, derive from the inexplicable jocularity of this "observer."

As can be seen, the author does not attempt to call the notion of reality into question. But, just in case, she prefers to have the most ordinary events communicated by "points of view" along the lines of the dwarf woman dying of laughter.

In "The Photographs," the untimely death is revealed amidst festivities and laughter. Hence the scandal, given that the most minimal decency demands a certain temporal and spatial discontinuity between a group of people fortified with numerous cups of cider and the sudden death of a little girl.

The conjunction of celebration, death, eroticism, and childhood emerges from a single, dazzling perspective which can be distinctly discerned in all of these tales.

Perhaps it might not be impossible to deduce a general characteristic now. ("Yes, if we choose to make it so, this leads directly to the cosmic." Lichtenberg.) The principal characteristic of *The Mortal Sin* consists of certain unions or alliances or links: laughter is not opposed to suffering; nor is love opposed to hate, celebration to death.

The existence of so many links obliges one to refer to "Celestina." This tale about an honest servant woman refers, I believe, to *La Celestina*, that extraordinary *voyeuse* (and "*oyeuse*") whose mercenary trade becomes the pretext for an absolute passion. Fernando de Rojas's creature succeeds in binding herself to pleasure by means of visual and auditory joy. The "Celestina" of Silvina Ocampo climaxes on hearing (or reading) of other people's misfortunes and deaths. The medieval lady colludes with eroticism; the modern maid, with death. Day after day, Celestina calls for dark nourishment, like the humor of the tale "Celestina." On the completion of her mourning portrait, they supply Celestina with faithful accounts of the rainbow; in this way, they kill her. A perfect murder or the multiplication of humor by sadism squared.

"Rhadamantos" is similar on account of its central

character: sinister, furtive, and irredeemably cruel. A tale to contemplate like a caricature, for example, the one with this beautiful title: Spite, "faithful beyond the grave."

"Autobiography of Irene" provides an example of suspiciously naive humor, but one should be mistrustful. Nearing her death, Irene thinks of the things she longed to see but never will. From the profusion of the universe she selects the essentials (for her), among which appear *the Columbus theater with its box seats and its desperate artists singing with one hand over their chest*. She who is about to die of guilt (or rather from the terror of her guilt) is sad because she will not have seen a tacky postcard.

In the tales of Silvina Ocampo, humor is almost always bound to arise from the level of the literal or, what is the same thing, from the simulacrum of asymbolism or, what is the same thing: one need only forget that language is made of symbols for the world to become a representation of The Great Asylum of the World.

> … and they drew many things. Everything that begins with M.
>
> —And why with M?—Alice inquired.
>
> —And why not?—said the March Hare.

The twenty stories that comprise *The Mortal Sin* are taken from Ocampo's various books. The careful selection of texts was undertaken by José Bianco. Nor is that all, and it's a shame. There is also a kind of preface, signed by no one, in which somebody repeats *reality*; *unreality*; *fantasy*. Through the repetition of these terms, the unnamed writer transcribes the phantom platitudes that characterize fantastic fiction. These unverifiable platitudes are in turn joined by complicit definitions. To say, for instance, that *the present selection of her stories highlights the de-realizing impulse of her style*, is to say very little, and what little it does say is untrue.

It is perhaps appropriate to transcribe a few luminous lines from Jorge Luis Borges:

> (…) I don't think we should talk about fantastic literature. And one of the reasons (…): since all literature is made of symbols, beginning with the letters and then the words, it is irrelevant whether those symbols are taken from the streets or from the imagination. That is, I believe that Macbeth is essentially (…) a character no less real than Rodion Raskolnikov…

WISE MEN AND POETS

HUMOR, ONE OF the continuous notes in *The Cheshire Cat*, would be more than enough to wear down *reality's copper coins.* * And Anderson Imbert multiplies this gift of humor by means of a singular reticence, the kind which is generally accompanied by extreme intellectualism. As soon as he has drawn attention to a certain aspect of reality (now absurd, now ominous), the author is pleased to concoct wise speculations with the apparent end of vindicating the absurd part as much as the adverse one—a rigorous and delicate method from which vertiginous conclusions derive. And rightly so, as the essence of humor is to corrode the world, or more precisely, to destroy its rigid structures, its stability, its weightiness.

As expressed by its greatest authors, modern humor is always metaphysical and poetic. Perhaps it inadvertently allows them to entrust it with a mission as privileged as it is painful: to ascertain the distance that separates us from reality. In this sense, and only in this sense, it is realistic, insofar as it delves to the very bottom of our notion of the absurd.

Despite this melancholy attribute, this is the most

---

* Italics indicate quotes from Anderson Imbert's *The Cheshire Cat*.

effective humor recorded in the history of literature. Nonetheless, it can happen—and it consistently does—that comedy turns against the comedian, and laughter turns against the reader or spectator. From this, a certain silence comes that seizes us, the silence that follows laughter and is markedly similar to the silence that propels (or prolongs) the moments of crisis in ancient tragedy. But it would hardly be surprising if the tragic were a sort of false bottom in the comic.

It should be added that a just appreciation of situations like the following is only possible from the peculiar standpoint of metaphysical and poetic humor:

> *They talked excitedly in the parlor.*
>
> *—I don't believe it—Estela interrupted, who until then had remained silent as she had not been born yet.*

A useful procedure in determining comic effects consists of pretending to forget the ambiguity of language in order to remain, inexorably, at the level of the literal. A valid example is provided by that gentleman in whom a secret has been confided and who promises: *I will be like the grave.* The commonplace is reanimated as if it were bewitched; he who formulated it is progressively modified; he is transformed, at last, into a grave.

(…)

… Anderson Imbert uses *black humor* to attest to the latent horror behind the mundane: An old woman is run over by a car, dies, gets up, takes a few steps, is run over again, dies, gets up, takes a few steps, is run over again, and it goes on like that forever. But this is not the worst of it; the cruel indifference demonstrated by passersby, bystanders, and motorists is more lamentable still. Caught in the hustle and bustle, none of them stops to contemplate the prodigious series of resurrections.

Poetic humor can gracefully intervene in the representation of a landscape:

It would have been possible (...) to see no one distinctly in the background of the landscape...

If one finds the black humor, be it poetic or metaphysical, the presence of "objective chance" will not appear strange:

He found a postcard in his pocket. He had never seen it. It wasn't addressed to him. Someone, in passing, had confused him with a mailbox. Or is it that he was a mailbox?

A question that approaches the transcendent problem which little Alice asks herself in order to find out if she, Alice, is Alice, or if she, Alice, is her little friend Mabel. The same wisdom prevails in the very short story just cited, from which one could infer the allusion to an ever-disturbing truth—the one that persuades us it takes very little, almost nothing, to strip the self of its deceptive pretense of being a finite thing, unchanging and immovable like a mailbox. At the same time, nobody has proven that the mailbox is located on a corner until the end of time. It is even valid to ask (after reading Anderson Imbert's story) if it really is a mailbox. It could well be a self, not a mailbox.

Because of his constitutional gift for humor, and because of his knowledge of the most diverse and subtle methods by which to express it, Enrique Anderson Imbert succeeds in effecting the coveted transformation of copper coins by means of a single gold one. To detail his procedures one by one would be an implausible task.

I conclude, then, with the theme of humor, but not before transcribing this outrageous situation:

From the benches we could only see the preacher's head above the tall lectern: when he smiled, his smile's corners split across the sides of his face, all the way around to the back of his head, and decapitated him. Then the head said...

(…)

The dizzying variety of themes in *The Cheshire Cat* includes fairytales and tales of "pink" humor. Perhaps most attractive are the ones in which the plot is the marvelous thing. The marvelous is (or would be) the completely unexpected intrusion of someone—of something—that eliminates the distance separating desire from reality.

THE HUMOR OF BORGES AND BIOY CASARES

> *First, I shall present an absurd description of the house; then I shall unsuccessfully attempt a crude and feeble portrait of its inhabitants.*
>
> —H. Bustos Domecq,
> *Six Problems for Don Isidro Parodi*

IN 1942, H. Bustos Domecq (the pseudonym of Jorge Luis Borges and Adolfo Bioy Casares) published a book of detective stories that belong to the genre of comedy: *Six Problems for Don Isidro Parodi*. Although the first edition had little impact, several months ago the publisher Sur reissued the book—a book unparalleled in the history of Spanish American literature. In all likelihood, the scant success of *Six Problems* was due to the exceeding subtlety and refinement of its humor, which could well have stupefied readers with a less developed comic sense. Furthermore, in order to enjoy this book one cannot be indifferent to the problems and mysteries of language because, ultimately, it is concerned with an exclusively verbal type of humor produced by two lovers of words. Quite rightly, Néstor Ibarra has thus categorized *Six Problems* as a "discourse on style."

The plot of the stories is interesting, but is not worth dwelling on, especially in a brief commentary. The book's preface is written by one of the main characters, as unimportant as the rest, given that none of them "exists;" nothing breathes in any of them which would lead one to think of living creatures. Quite the opposite: they are creatures of language. It is for this reason that the book creates the same effect as, for example, those of Raymond Queneau. It is impossible to refer it to anything outside of it; the characters and events exist and unfold solely by the force of the language that sustains them.

The characters are as follows: two *compadritos*,* an old-fashioned man of letters, an avant-garde poet and his disciple, a hispanist, a Chinese diplomat, two high society ladies, and a detective who lives in jail by virtue of the simple fact that he is imprisoned. As Gervasio Montenegro states in the prologue: *the honor of being the first detective behind bars goes to Don Isidro.* Borges has studied the satiric value of such inventions in his "Art of the Insult:"

> One of the satirical traditions (not scorned by Macedonio Fernández, Quevedo, or George Bernard Shaw) is the unqualified inversion of terms. According to this celebrated recipe, doctors are inevitably accused of promulgating infection and death, notaries of theft, executioners of promoting longevity, and adventure stories of anaesthetizing or putting the reader to sleep...

On a first reading, we think that Borges and Bioy Casares have imitated the language of various social and cultural groups in Argentina. A more attentive re-reading shows that, in fact, the authors have utilized these various spoken and written styles, exaggerating them into a range of spoken and written styles that no one ever uses in the so-called *real world*. That is, the habits of speech and writing particular to

---

* Italics refer to quotes from H. Bustos Domecq's *Six Problems for Don Isidro Parodi*.

each figure in the book have been transmuted into autonomous literary material. It will be said that this is an obvious aspect of the writer's craft. True, but in this case it must be emphasized due to Borges and Bioy Casares' extraordinary gift for "contemplating" language with virgin eyes. Many of the turns of phrase, usages, and expressions which we apply to speech and writing appear either exceedingly funny or pregnant with poetic significance if we consider them with fresh eyes and ears. And this is the miracle of Borges and Bioy Casares's verbal humor: to present us with several common elements of speech within a context that renders them foreign, to abruptly defamiliarize everyday language such that it becomes suddenly *other*—it is right in front of us and it is grotesque, delicious, absurd. Naturally, it makes us laugh. But it also allows us to discover it anew.

The characters' inability to communicate with each other is absolute. Nobody understands anything about anyone. This is where misunderstandings arise: failing to grasp the meaning, both of others' actions and of their own, each character proceeds to narrate those actions (as Don Isidro is the only person who understands them, these narratives always occur in his cell) as if they were utterly meaningless. This disjunction between cause and effect is another source of comedy. Its counterpart is the complicity the authors establish with the reader. For example:

I don't know where Naples is, but if someone doesn't clear this matter up, it'll bury you like Vesuvius in ways you can't begin to imagine.

HIGH COMEDY NOT only impugns the reality it points to; it also impugns the comedian himself. It follows that among its many happily warped styles one should be that of Borges himself. Because beneath all the hilarious circumstances narrated by these outrageous voices lies the eternal false bottom of laughter: the tragic. *Six Problems for Don Isidro Parodi* is a book populated by entertaining puppets. Yet while those puppets amuse us, they are also useful instruments of condemnation, attack, and counter-attack. It is often said that to err is human, but to laugh divine. And you have to wonder whether Christ himself wouldn't have laughed at the image of a camel passing through the eye of a needle.

A TRADITION OF RUPTURE

CUADRIVIO BRINGS TOGETHER four essays on four poets:
Rubén Darío, Ramón López Velarde, Fernando Pessoa,
and Luis Cernuda. Far from seeking out random similari-
ties between them, Octavio Paz presents them each as singular, distinct, and irreplaceable; that is, he presents them
as they were. Nevertheless, the works of these poets share
something in common: their *rupture with the immediate tradition** and, what is more, their *construction of a tradition of
rupture* which is precisely *the tradition of our modern poetry*.

At the beginning of his essay on López Velarde, Paz
relates its genesis: *I set out, once again, to interrogate these
poems—as one interrogates oneself—*. This is his critical approach: a dialogue with the work of poetry, a dialogue that
excludes nothing, from the historical moment that dates the
work to the silence that breathes in it. Paz doesn't explain:
he searches, explores, interrogates (not only the poet he is
in dialogue with but also himself, the one asking the questions), and his essays show these movements; they recount
these enthralling adventures of the spirit inseparable from
existence.

---

* Italics indicate quotes from Paz's *Cuadrivio*.

Modernismo *and Rubén Darío*

PAZ BEGINS WITH an exhaustive analysis of the word *modernismo* which Rubén Darío and his friends constantly employed from 1888 on. With this word, they declared their tenacious will to be modern. This pretension to modernity probably appears superficial. It is not if you imagine, with Paz, that the *modernistas'* desire to be modern was a desire to insert themselves in living history, in the now, in the present. This yearning proves that they felt outside of living history or the present, since no one wants to enter the place they already are. Paz observes that the distance between Latin America and Europe, diminished thanks to technological advances, increased their historical distance. *To go to Paris or London wasn't to go to another continent but to leap into another century.* In this regard, *modernismo* has been defined as a longing to escape from Latin American reality. Paz affirms the opposite. He understands that what the *modernistas* wanted—those writers for whom modernity and cosmopolitanism were synonymous—was *a Latin America contemporary with Paris and London.*

Paz refers on multiple occasions to the *modernistas'* fascination with the plurality apparent in space and time. The famous lines: "and very eighteenth-century / and very modern, / audacious, cosmopolitan…" constitute, among others, a sufficient example of this magnetic attraction. The irony isn't lost on Paz that the first authentically Latin American literary movement would declare itself, mere moments after its birth, as cosmopolitan, and ask itself what that Cosmopolis was called. Undoubtedly its name is the same as that of every city, which is to say, of none. This is why he asserts: Modernismo *is an abstract passion, even though its poets take pleasure in accumulating all kinds of strange objects.* Objects that are signs—but signs can be erased or replaced—and not symbols. What is certain is that *modernismo*'s brilliant decorative excesses scarcely manage to conceal the horror of the void and, above all, an intense hunger for presence even stronger than their thirst for the present.

It therefore comes as no surprise when Paz describes *modernismo* as *a nihilist aesthetic*. Yet while this nihilism is sooner suffered than confronted, the best poets of the movement—Darío first and foremost—are aware of the emptiness of their search (of its rootlessness, meaning its lack of a past, and thus, of a future), since *that search, if it is a search for something and not mere dissipation, is nostalgia for an origin*.

It is not by chance when he examines the reforms carried out by the *modernistas*, whether they have to do with syntax, prosody, or the vocabulary of our language, Paz dwells with particular aptness on prosody. To be sure, *modernismo was a prodigious exploration of the rhythmic possibilities of our language*. This exploration leads it to renew the tradition of irregular versification, which is as old as the Spanish language itself. To that it adds the resurrection of accentual rhythm and the invention of new meters. But to go back to the rhythm: the most notable part of this difficult and magnificent exploration whose end was to acquire a modern, cosmopolitan language, is that it revealed to the *modernistas* the authentic tradition of Spanish poetry. And this is how, through indirection and guided by necessity, these poets rediscovered the Hispanic tradition, the true one, *the central and most ancient one*, the one unknown to purists. "To have gathered from the air a live tradition," reads a line by Pound. Traditionalists know little about this universal current. It is *the same principle that governs the works of the great romantics and symbolists: rhythm as a source of poetic creation*.

In this way, the *modernistas* not only recover the Spanish tradition, they also add to it something which hadn't existed before. It is in this last sense that Paz asserts that *modernismo is a true beginning*. One such example might be Darío's line: *Love your rhythm and rhythm your actions*, of which Paz observes that never before had poetry written in Spanish attempted to express words of this kind—words that discover in rhythm *an entryway—not to salvation but to the reconciliation of man and the cosmos*.

What is more, there is another idea, equally foreign until then to poetry in our language, which breathes in *modernismo* and consists in thinking of poetry as a way of becoming sacred, a kind of revelation distinct from the religious one. *It is the original revelation, the true beginning.* This reconstruction of the divine by means of poetry is particular to modern poetry. From here—Paz notes—comes the modernity of *modernismo*.

It is worth bearing in mind that Darío exegetes and commentators tend to ignore a crucially important detail that Paz is quick to highlight at the beginning of this essay: Rubén Darío was the first, outside of France, to discover the "Uruguayan, never French," Comte de Lautréamont at a time when he was virtually unknown in France itself.

If Rubén Darío *is modernismo*, it is also certain that, like every great poet, he belongs more to the history of literature than to any particular style.

With few exceptions, poets of the Spanish language never appear to have endured those confrontations with human speech in which it reveals itself as the "musician of silence." In the essay that Paz devotes to Darío, one finds these perfect lines: *Language is the expression of self-consciousness, which is the consciousness of the fall. Through the wound of signification, the full being which is the poem bleeds out and becomes prose: description and interpretation of the world.*

It is important to know whether Darío was aware of

these truths that Paz expresses with such extraordinary beauty. Or, said another way: Was Darío aware of words' ambiguity, of their powers, of their risks? That is how Paz depicts him. On the one hand, for Darío, the poet belongs to "the race that creates life with Pythagorean numbers." According to this phrase, the poet possesses the gift of fashioning the words that form the world—that erect, word by word, *a magical double of the cosmos*—words which on recovering their original being, become music. Yet Darío knows that the word is not only music, but also meaning, and that the same distance which separates man from the world separates the word from the thing it names. This is why Paz also describes the poet as "the awareness of our human clay." Darío, like almost all the great modern poets, continually oscillated between the two extremes of the word: music and meaning.

Furthermore, in Darío's particular case, duality—which in his first books only manifests aesthetically—reveals itself in *Songs of Life and Hope* and after *in its human truth, as a splitting of the soul*. Nothing attests more accurately to this duality than the symbols by which the poet expresses himself. Paz observes that Darío inevitably recurs to symbols belonging to one of two spaces, the aerial and the aquatic:

> To the first belong the heavens, the light, the stars and—by analogy or sympathetic magic—the metaphysical half of the universe: the nameless, incorruptible realm of ideas, music, and numbers. The second is the domain of the blood, the heart, the sea, wine, woman, the passions, and—also by magical transmission—the jungle, its animals, and its monsters.

Two verses by Paz himself read: "between I am and you are, / the word *bridge*." Poetry is, among other things, a reconciliation: a bridge between the jungle and the stars, a union between animals and music. This is how Darío perceived it, for whom poetry was *vision, which in itself is a fusion of the cosmic duality.*

If, for Darío, the poem is the place where oppositions coalesce and reconcile, so too is the body of woman. Paz's dazzling analysis of his *erotic mysticism* may well be the most important part of the essay. A few lines by way of example:

> *The story of his heart is plural in two senses—because of the number of women he loved and because of his fascination with the plurality of the cosmos. For the Platonic poet, the apprehension of reality is a gradual shift from the multiple to the one; love consists of the progressive disappearance of the universe's seeming heterogeneity. Darío understands this heterogeneity as the proof or manifestation of unity: every form is at once a complete world and a part of the totality. Unity is not one, but rather a universe of universes, impelled by erotic gravitation: instinct, passion. Darío's eroticism is a magical vision of the world.*

And later:

> *Darío's imagination tends to manifest in contradictory and complementary directions, and this is the source of his dynamism. One vision of woman—as extension, as sacred animal passivity (clay, ambrosia, earth, bread)—gives way to another: woman as "the power shadows fear, the dark queen."*

This second vision continues to evoke the *dark lady of the tomb and the house of the dead.* At the same time, it is significant that Darío refers to death as She and that his attitude toward Her is ambiguous and entirely erotic: she terrifies him yet he waits for her like a lover. On the one hand, death is the unknown that stalks him from the shadows, and on the other, it is an object of desire promising unknown and overwhelming delights. *Death was his Medusa and his siren. A death which was dualistic, like everything he touched, saw, and sang. Unity is always two.*

Ramón López Velarde

IN THE WORK of López Velarde, the quotidian suffers a *fortunate metamorphosis*: the most humble, everyday things, from utensils to trash, are preserved in the space of the poem and, as a result, redeemed. Rejecting the utilitarian standards that restrict things to their use and consumption, the poet takes those same things into the poem and renders them other.

This metamorphosis is the work of metaphor. Metaphor *is the agent of change; its mode of action is the embrace.* Few poets have possessed such an acute awareness of *our lack of being*, of the fact that actual reality only appears to us in privileged moments, if at all. The function of metaphor, then, is *to be the equivalent or analogic double of such states of exception—whence its density, its apparent obscurity, and its paradoxes.* Indeed, López Velarde is *a difficult poet who proclaims a difficult aesthetic.* He finds his language in the familiar, not the foreign: he prefers the most available, most self-evident words, so evident that at times they blind us with their excess of evidence. He doesn't strive to surprise; more than anything, he yearns for honesty, for the non-alienated language he discovers in everyday speech. To be sure, such discoveries are not a given, but a conquest, a tracing back to the roots of words long debased by excessive use in order to recover their former purity.

Paz reveals the extent to which expression, for López Velarde, is synonymous with inner knowledge, and even more so *with self-creation.* To write is to configure one's very being: the poet knows himself by naming himself, and he only learns of his deepest feelings by expressing them in words. And because he stakes his identity on these words, they must be absolutely precise, absolutely just, absolutely faithful. Furthermore, by naming himself, he steps outside the I and, with that motion, he is and exists in unparalleled fullness (recall López Velarde's insight about our deficiency of being). Paz thus concludes: *He cares about adjectives because he cares about his soul.*

But the most valuable feature of this essay is its extended analysis of the correlation between the Provençal troubadours' conception of passionate love and the sense of love as it manifests in the Mexican poet's life and work. From this extremely convincing parallel, it follows that López Velarde's two loves *correspond exactly with the Lady of the Provençal lyric tradition.* Moreover, and most importantly, this sort of passion defines López Velarde's personal drama—*being in love with love, with the Image rather than an actual, mortal creature.*

Against such absolute and dangerously unbounded love is López Velarde's attempt—perfectly achieved—to incorporate into the poem everything traditional poetry had historically disparaged as trivial or passé. Thus, in spite of his utterly unreal sense of love and in spite of his uncommonly intense identification of love with death and the deceased, Paz can say: *The bond he establishes between the world and himself is amorous in nature: the embrace, the metaphor of affection.* That embrace, in addition to being the poet's lifeline, is also what gives many of his poems their enduring beauty and living presence. One example is the passage Paz quotes in which López Velarde describes his presentiment of de Chirico's paintings—paintings he never actually saw: *the lost steps of consciousness, the falling of a glove down a metaphysical well...*

Fernando Pessoa

DEVOID OF ANY memorable or surprising events, Pessoa's biography is necessarily tenuous. About his emotional life, we only know of a brief love affair which he broke off in a letter stating that his fate "obeys another Law, whose existence you couldn't begin to imagine…" These words, or the sense of the impossible they reveal, persistently call to mind the work of Kierkegaard and Kafka. But even if they do him honor, it is best avoid comparisons as Pessoa's case is utterly unique in the history of literature. Nor is it useful to classify him in terms of his connection to the dark arts, a connection he shares with other great modern poets from Nerval, Mallarmé, and Rimbaud, to Breton. Paz's definition, by contrast, is very apt: the story of the real Pessoa *could be reduced to the passage between the unreality of his everyday life and the reality of his fictions*.

The following description is also very true:

> In the Portuguese poet Fernando Pessoa, we recognize the pride of Hegel and the philosophers of nature, the exemplary attitude of the idealist thinker who knows that nothing is impossible for the human spirit, not even the power to create life. For this man at once possessed and miraculously free (insofar as he toys with his possessors), the poetic act is verified by its genesis in the central abyss of one's being, which breaks through its restraints to attempt a fabulous and ever-renewing quest: to tear the Other out of itself, to dress it in living flesh and, casting it into space, to give it its chances.

Pessoa not only gave life to the Other, but also to Others. In 1914, the heteronyms break forth; Pessoa gives birth to the poets who are and are not Pessoa, despite the fact that he created them. They are Alberto Caeiro and his disciples, Álvaro de Campos, and Ricardo Reis. ("Of course, I'm not sure if they're the ones that don't exist or if I'm the nonexistent one. In such cases, we shouldn't be dogmatic.") In terms of their poems, they have little to no relationship with one another, nor are they similar to those of Fernando

Pessoa himself. Each poet, whether he be called Caeiro, Campos, or Reis, commands his own style and exists unto himself. Moreover, not only do they not resemble Pessoa, their creator, they even contradict him. In short, Pessoa *is not an inventor of poet-characters but rather the creator of works-of-poets.*

Alberto Caeiro is the master—of Campos, of Reis, and of Pessoa himself (in a letter describing the origin of the heteronyms, Pessoa writes: "What followed was the appearance of someone in me, someone I immediately named Alberto Caeiro. Pardon the absurdity of my statement: my master appeared in me.")

Caeiro is the man reconciled with nature. He lacks ideas because he denies them. His function is to exist; his belief: *what exists just is.* Paz characterizes him as an *innocent poet*, as Caeiro speaks from a place anterior to any division. For him, words are things and, by contrast with Pessoa, he has no nostalgia for unity (how could he have nostalgia for the domain he inhabits?). Although his words are those of a wise man, Paz rightly asserts that *the mask of innocence Caeiro shows us is not wisdom; to be wise is to resign oneself to the knowledge that we are not innocent. Pessoa, who knew this, was closer to wisdom.*

The futurist Álvaro de Campos is also distinct from his master. Their only resemblances lie in the fact that *both of them write in free verse, both ride roughshod over Portuguese, and neither avoids clichés.*

Anyone who has read the Futurists' manifestos and the poems by the movement's various members can confirm the confident and even triumphalist tone of those champions of the modern city. The peculiarity of Campos is that, with the same voice as that of the Futurists—as well as an aftertaste of Whitman—, he sings a song of defeat, of agony and impotence. "By the painful light of the factory's huge electric lamps / I feverishly write. / I write gnashing my teeth rabid before this beauty, / This beauty utterly unknown to the ancients."

Ricardo Reis is a very different poet from Caeiro and Campos. Neoclassical, he writes short pagan odes. Pessoa is no great admirer of his formal perfection: "Reis writes better than I, but with a purism I consider exaggerated." For his part, Reis writes critical notes on Caeiro and Campos *which are a model of verbal precision and aesthetic incomprehension.* Reis, like Pessoa, draws on fixed forms and meters. His poetry—like Pessoa's—is a search for his own identity. *Both lose themselves in the intricacies of their thought, culminate in a twist and, merging with themselves, embrace a shadow. The poem is not the expression of being but rather a memorial for that moment of fusion.*

The work of Pessoa himself consists of writings in prose and poetry in both Portuguese and English (these last are the least important). For their part, the prose writers are divided among those signed with his ownname and those bearing the pseudonyms of the Baron of Teive and Bernardo Soares (Pessoa notes that there is no reason to consider these two names as heteronyms since they write in his style).

In the work of Pessoa, *the theme of alienation and the search for oneself, whether in the enchanted forest or in the abstract city, is something more than a theme: it is the very substance of his work.*

For Pessoa, the poet is *a pretender who pretends so completely he ends up pretending that the pain he honestly feels is pain.* Such faith in the unreal leads him to say: "Why do I, the deceived, still judge that what is mine is mine?" Propositions like these are something more than paradoxes infused with the kind of painful and delicious humor that calls to mind a Lichtenberg or a Macedonio Fernández. They are, as Paz shows, the key to the meaning of the heteronyms.

The heteronyms are what Pessoa wanted to be, but they are also what he did not want to be, an I, an individual personality. Therefore, this process of disintegration, both endured and assumed by Pessoa with an originality and a bravery rarely equaled, creates a *secret fertility*: the I ends by being corroded. And this isn't a bad thing if we share Octavio Paz's conviction that *the I is the true desert, not only because it encloses us in ourselves and thus condemns us to live with a ghost, but also because it withers everything it touches.*

Luis Cernuda

CERNUDA IS THE poet of love. This assertion implies the acceptance of a commonplace. Nevertheless, Paz warns us not to forget that for Cernuda—as for André Gide—it was a binding moral necessity *not* to sidestep the Uranian nature of his passion. No hidden subversive intent motivated these demands for sincerity. Rather, they must be attributed to Cernuda's valiant love of truth (in addition to being a great poet, Cernuda was *one of the few moralists Spain has ever produced*). In Paz's view, to deny the nature of Cernuda's love is to misunderstand the significance of his work, just as one fails to truly understand the work by thinking it entirely depends on one specific passion. As for that passion, it forces him to feel excluded but not condemned: *His is* a different truth *one which separates him from the world; yet that same truth, in a second movement, leads him to discover another truth which is both personal and universal.*

Cernuda is the poet of love. Nothing is more certain, nothing more complicated. In addition to speaking of love, he also speaks of "*desire*," of pleasure, and, at the same time, of solitude. These are the central themes of his work. And given that he titles that work *Reality and Desire*, there is no doubt that the theme of desire was of principle importance to Cernuda. Paz points out that *the fate of the word* desire, *from Baudelaire through Breton, is inextricable from that of poetry.* It follows that defining desire will become as impossible as defining poetry. But what matters here is to understand what Cernuda's poems say about desire. Paz shows that they say something genuinely terrifying—that insofar as desire is real, reality is not; that *desire makes the imaginary real, and reality unreal.* But how is this possible? Because desire expresses itself in images that rush to inhabit the world, dislodge the living beings there, and take their place. As for love, it is the only force that can conduct the passage of desire into reality and raise an erotic object to the level of the beloved. A conflict emerges, however, between desire and love: desire *seeks consummation through the destruction of its object; love reveals that its object is indestructible…and irreplaceable.*

Another idea of Cernuda's: love exists outside us and only uses us to materialize. This tendency toward the side of abstraction (even if that abstraction calls itself love and commands its own energies) bespeaks a conviction that accords little value to man. That is, what little value we have rests in our mortal condition, mortality being a synonym for flux and death. And while it may be true that few poets have glorified the human body with such ardor, the human face never once appears in Cernuda's poems. Paz explains this exclusion: for Cernuda, a beautiful young body is *a cipher of the universe* (…), *a solar system, a nucleus of physical and psychic radiation.* In other words, for an instant the body incarnates a marvelous force beyond itself. Paz is well aware that these ideas mean ignorance of the other, *a contemplation of "that which is loved," not the lover.*

There is a beautiful precision to Cernuda's discovery that *each time we love, we lose ourselves: we are other.* It is not the individual self that is fulfilled in love but rather its aspiration to otherness.

Another thing that Cernuda's poems tell us (and that the works of many poets, both ancient and modern, also tell us)—is that love violently contradicts the social order. And this does not refer, as some might easily assume, to the particular nature of his love but to all true love. To love is to transgress.

A poet of love. Yes, because he exalted it as almost no one else has. And this is ultimately the truth in which he believed: *not the truth of man but the truth of love*.

Cernuda also exalted nature, which revealed herself to him as the mother of the gods and of myth. In addition, she offered him a safeguard against human flux. Of course, nature is also in flux, but within her harmonious changes she remains identical with herself. As Paz describes Cernuda's landscapes: *Now and again they are arrested in time and the light in them thinks as it does in certain paintings by Turner.*

Was Cernuda ever reconciled with the human condition, comprised as it is of time that runs out? Paz discerns three ways of accessing time in his poems: the one Cernuda refers to as *concord* signifies union with the sovereign instant (manifest perfection and fullness, suddenly present, here and now, whether by means of a landscape, a body, or a piece of music). In contrast, the second way or perspective requires distance: *man does not fuse with external reality but his gaze creates a space of revelation between reality and his consciousness.* The third way is the vision of human creations, others' as well as his own. By this last way, Cernuda becomes aware of his participation in history and—what is especially important in his case—of what man should achieve: the metamorphosis of time's absurd, blind passage into living, significant time, that is, time transmuted into works and actions.

This and much more is revealed to an exceptional reader such as Octavio Paz by *Reality and Desire*, a book encompassing every stage of Cernuda's life, with the exception of childhood. The secret of this work's fascination lies, as Paz shows, in a double movement of simultaneous absorption in the poem and reflection on what it expresses. In Cernuda, reflection creates a species of grave but inviting distance which is like a space filled with exquisite silence— the silence that precedes the language of accuracy and truth and without which words are merely babble or a whisper.

Cernuda reflected extensively on language, something very rare in the Spanish tradition. He was concerned, above all, with the relationships between the written and the spoken word. What is more, he attempted to write as we speak.

The distinction Paz makes between a spoken language and a popular language is important in this regard. Spoken language is the language of the great city which modern poetry has drawn on since Baudelaire. By contrast, popular language, *if indeed it really exists and isn't an invention of German romanticism, is the residue of feudal times. Its cult is a cult of nostalgia.*

Cernuda's *different truth* is embodied in a poetics that is no less different. If one were to ask what place this poet holds in modern Spanish-language poetry, then Paz's response would be the following: *If the place Cernuda occupies in our modern poetry could be defined in two sentences, I would say that he is the poet who speaks, not for everyone, but for all the single individuals we are. And he wounds us at the very core of this single individual, "which is not called fortune, fame, or glory," but rather* the truth of ourselves.

Paz's dialogue with works of poetry is impossible to transpose in a brief account, not only because of the new meanings he constantly enriches them with, but also because of his captivating prose, which discourages all attempts to reduce it to another language. It takes enormous courage and freedom to rethink, for oneself, works that have already been the object of every analysis and interpretation, as is the case with the work of Rubén Darío, and even of López Velarde. But Paz has said, in a different book, that the great contemporary poets are also great critics. *Cuadrivio* and the other books of criticism by the great poet Octavio Paz attest to the truth of this assertion.

COMMENTARIES

Prologues for an Anthology of Young Argentine Poets

"The Poet and the Poem" dated Paris, December 1962.
First published in *Quince poetas*. Ed. César Magrini (Buenos Aires: Ediciones Centurión, 1968). Republished in Alejandra Pizarnik, *El deseo de la palabra* [*Desire for the Word*] (Barcelona: Ocnos, 1975).

"The Poem and its Reader" dated Buenos Aires, 1967.
First published in *Quince poetas*. Republished in *El deseo de la palabra*.

Attempt at a Prologue in Their Style, Not Mine

Undated.
First published in Alejandra Pizarnik, *Prosa completa* [*Complete Prose*] (Barcelona: Lumen, 2012).

Notes for an Interview

Four typed pages, hand-corrected by Pizarnik.
First published in *Prosa completa*.

[unexpected]— In brackets as a possible variant from a posthumously published version of Pizarnik's manuscript, which was unfinished at the time of her death.

Interview for *El Pueblo*, Córdoba (April 17, 1967)

One-page typescript, hand-corrected by Pizarnik.
First published in *Prosa completa*.

Adolfo Bioy Casares (1914-1999) — an Argentine fiction writer, journalist, translator, and frequent collaborator of Jorge Luis Borges. Olga Orozco (1920-1999) was an Argentine poet, journalist, and a member of the surrealist-influenced "Tercera Vanguardia" [Third Vanguard] or "Generation of 1940." Enrique Molina (1910-1997) was an Argentine poet and painter deeply influenced by surrealism. Silvina Ocampo (1903-1993) was an Argentine poet, fiction writer, and collaborator of both Borges and her husband, Bioy Casares. Juan Rulfo (1917-1986) was a Mexican fiction writer, screenwriter, and photographer, best known for his collection of short stories, *El llano en llamas* [*The Burning Plain*] (1953), and his novel *Pedro Páramo* (1955).

8 Questions for Women Writers, Actors, Scientists, Artistst, Social Workers, and Journalists

First published in *Sur* 326 (Buenos Aires, September 1970-June 1971).

"When the endless servitude of woman is broken, when ... we will understand them." — "Quand sera brisé l'infini servage de la femme, quand elle vivra pour elle et par elle, l'homme—jusqu'ici abominable—, lui ayant donné son renvoi, elle sera poète, elle aussi! La femme trouvera de l'inconnu! Ses mondes d'idées différeront-ils des nôtres? —Elle trouvera des choses étranges, insondables, repoussantes, délicieuses; nous les prendrons, nous les comprendrons" (Letter from Rimbaud to Paul Demeny. Charleville, 15/V/1871). *Rimbaud: Complete Works, Selected Letters.* Trans. Wallace Fowlie. U of Chicago P, 1966. 309. French in original.

"Change life." — "Changer la vie." Arthur Rimbaud, "Délires 1: Vierge Folle–L'Époux Infernal" ["Delirium 1: The Foolish Virgin–The Infernal Bridegroom"], *Une Saison en Enfer* [*A Season in Hell*] (1873). French in original.

Some Keys to Alejandra Pizarnik

Interview by Martha Isabel Moia.
First published in *El deseo de la palabra*.

For well I know where flows the fount — A reference to the sixteenth-century poem "Cantar del alma que se huelga de conocer a Dios por fe" ["Song of the soul that rejoices in knowing God through faith"] by Saint John of the Cross.

"I am [inhabited]; I speak to who-I-was and who-I-was speaks to me. (…) One isn't alone in one's skin." — "Je suis [habité]; je parle à qui-je-fus et qui-je-fus me parlent. (…) On n'est pas seul dans sa peau." Henri Michaux, *Qui je fus* [*Who I Was*] (1927). Pizarnik omits the word "habité" [inhabited]. French in original.

Customs Agent's — A reference to the French painter Henri Julien Félix Rousseau (1844-1910).

Humor and Poetry in Julio Cortázar's
Cronopios and Famas

Dated 1961.
First published in *Revista Nacional de Cultura* 25.160 (Caracas, September-October 1963). Republished in *El deseo de la palabra*.

This essay references Julio Cortázar's *Historias de cronopios y de famas* (Buenos Aires: Ediciones Minotauro, 1962). Pizarnik's quotations from the book appear in italics.

Archpriest of Hita — The medieval Castilian poet Juan Ruiz (c. 1283-c. 1350), best known for his poem *Libro de Buen Amor* [*The Book of Good Love*].

Cancha Rayada — In the second battle of Cancha Rayada (Chile, 1818), South American revolutionaries were defeated by Spanish royalists.

Various Accounts of South American Events,
People, and Things (Sixteenth-Century Texts)

First published in *Cuadernos* (Paris, 1964).

This essay addresses the collection *Relación varia de hechos, hombres y cosas de estas Indias Meridionales. Textos del siglo XVI* (Buenos Aires: Losada, 1963). Pizarnik's quotations from the book appear in italics.

Pietro Aretino — Italian poet, playwright, and satirist known for the licentiousness of his writings (1492-1556).

Silences in Motion

First published in *Sur* 294 (May-June 1965).

This essay references Héctor Álvarez Murena's *El demonio de la armonía* [*The Demon of Harmony*] (Buenos Aires: Sur, 1964). Pizarnik's quotations from the book appear in italics.

H.A. Murena (1923-1975) — A prolific Argentine writer, a frequent contributor to the journal *Sur*, and the first Spanish translator of Walter Benjamin's works.

"who knows the void better than the dead." — "qui sur le néant en sait plus que les morts." Stéphane Mallarmé, "Angoisse" ["Anguish"], in *Poésies* [*Poems*] (1899). French in original.

Alberto Girri's *The Eye*

First published in *Sur* 291 (November-December 1964).

This essay is about Alberto Girri's novel, *El ojo* (Buenos Aires: Losada, 1964). Pizarnik's quotations from the novel appear in italics.

Alberto Girri (1919-1991) — An Argentine poet and contributor to the journals *Sur* and *La Nación*. The author of some 30 books, Girri's translations were also influential in drawing Argentine readers' attention to English-language poets including T.S. Eliot, Wallace Stevens, and William Carlos Williams.

Epigraph — "*...où (...) le passé et le future (...) cessent d'être perçus contradictoirement.*" André Breton, *Second manifeste du Surréalisme* [*Second Manifesto of Surrealism*] (1929). French in original.

"as with leaves, so with the lives of men" — Pizarnik refers to Book VI of *The Iliad*: "As is the generation of leaves, so is that of humanity. / The winds scatter the leaves on the ground, but the live timber / burgeons with leaves again in the season of spring returning. / So one generation of men will grow while another / dies." *The Iliad of Homer*. Trans. Richmond Lattimore. (Chicago: U of Chicago P, 1951).

"I stand before this feminine land / Like a child before the fire."
— "Je suis devant ce paysage feminin / Comme un enfant devant
le feu." Paul Éluard, "L'extase" ["Ecstacy"], in *Derniers Poèmes
d'amour* [*Last Love Poems*] (1963). French in original.

Epigraph — "*Toute parole étant idée...*" Arthur Rimbaud. Letter
to Paul Démeny (Charleville, May 15, 1871). French in
original.

"bitter knowledge" — "amer savoir." An allusion to Charles
Baudelaire's "Le Voyage" ["The Voyage"] in *Les Fleurs du Mal* [*The
Flowers of Evil*] (1857). French in original.

Epigraph — "*Chez lui, entre le regard et la parole persiste une relation nuptiale.*" Gabriel Honoré Marcel, *Homo Viator* (1945).
French in original.

Simón Cireneo — the man compelled to bear Jesus's cross as he
was led to Golgotha.

A Ricardo Molinari Anthology

First published in *Zona Franca* 2.26 (October 1965).

This essay references Ricardo Molinari's book, *Un día, el tiempo,
las nubes* [*Day, Time, Clouds*] (Buenos Aires: Sur, 1965). Pizarnik's
quotations from the book appear in italics.

Ricardo Molinari (1898-1996) — An Argentine poet originally
associated with the Buenos Aires-based "Grupo Florida" ["Florida
Group"]. In 1958, Molinari received Argentina's National Poetry
Prize for his book *Unida noche* [*United Night*] and, in 1968, he
was inducted into the Argentine Academy of Letters.

"a deliciously-scented garment woven by fairies" — "un habit
tissé par les fées et d'une délicieuse odeur." Gérard de Nerval, in
Aristide Marie, *Gérard de Nerval: le Poète et L'Homme* [*Gérard de
Nerval: His Life and Work*] (1914). French in original.

"Enough, sir harp" — Pizarnik combines two lines from Canto
III of Vicente Huidobro's *Altazor* (1931): "Basta señora arpa de
las bellas imágenes" ["Enough, madame harp of the beautiful

images"] and "Basta señor violin hundido en una ola ola" ["Enough, sir violin sunk in a wave wave"].

"**I also take very seriously ... that which one could very well excuse...**" — Garcilaso de la Vega, "A la muy manífica señora doña Jerónima Palova de Almogávar" (1534).

A Difficult Balance: *Zona Franca*

First published in *Sur* 297 (November-December 1965).

This essay discusses the monthly Caracas-based literary magazine *Zona Franca* [*Free Zone*]. Pizarnik's quotes from the magazine appear in italics.

Guillermo Sucre (b. 1933)— A Venezuelan poet, literary critic, and translator, best known for his work on Borges.

Re-Reading Breton's *Nadja*

First published in *Testigo* 5 (Buenos Aires, January-March 1970). Previously published under a different title in *Imagen* 32 (Caracas, 1968). Republished in *El deseo de la palabra*.

This essay focuses on André Breton's iconic surrealist novel *Nadja* (1928). Pizarnik's quotes from *Nadja* appear in italics.

Epigraph — "*J'ai délaissé sans remords d'adorables suppliantes.*" André Breton, "Le Surréalism et la peinture" ["Surrealism and Painting"] (1928). French in original.

to haunt — *hanter*. French in original.

Epigraph — "*Et c'est toujours la seule...*" Gérard de Nerval, "Artemis," in *Les Chimères* (1854).

Beauty — *La beauté*. French in original

dream of stone — *rêve de pierre*. French in original.

madwoman — *détraquée*. French in original.

sorceress — *magicienne*. French in original.

"Dream of her; she will give no other answer." — From the final lines of Hölderlin's poem "An die Natur" ["On Nature"] (1795).

trop tard — *never more*

never more — English in original.

André Pieyre de Mandiargues's *The Motorcycle*

First published in *Sur* 320 (September-October 1969).

Pizarnik is reviewing André Pieyre de Mandiargues's novel *La Motocicleta* (Barcelona: Seix Barral, 1968).

André Pieyre de Mandiargues (1909-1991) — A French novelist, essayist, poet, and playwright associated with Surrealism and best known for the controversial eroticism of his work.

Note on Julio Cortázar's "The Other Heaven"

Dated 1967.
First published in *La vuelta a Cortázar en nueve ensayos* (Buenos Aires: Carlos Pérez, 1968). Republished in *El deseo de la palabra*.

This essay addresses Cortázar's short story, "El otro cielo," which appeared in *Todos los fuegos el fuego* [*All Fires the Fire*] (Buenos Aires: Sudamericana, 1966). Pizarnik's quotations from the story appear in italics.

Epigraph — "*Enfant, certains ciels ont affiné mon optique...*" Arthur Rimbaud, "Guerre" ["War"], in *Les Illuminations* [*Illuminations*] (1895). French in original.

"as simple as a musical phrase" — Ibid.

"mental traveler" — A reference to William Blake's poem "The Mental Traveler," translated into Spanish by Pablo Neruda in 1935.

"dreadful accusation" — This phrase and the following two passages in quotation marks refer to: Comte de Lautréamont, *Les Chants de Maldoror* [*The Songs of Maldoror*] (1868-1869).

the sinister — Enrique Pichon Rivière, "Lo maravilloso y lo siniestro en la obra del conde de Lautréamont" [The Marvelous and the Sinister in the Work of the Count of Lautréamont"]. *Revista de Psicoanálisis* [*Journal of Psychoanalysis*] (Buenos Aires, May 1945). Pizarnik's note.

"one dies of less." — *on meurt à moins.* See Pizarnik's poem "Vértigos o contemplación de algo que termina" ["Vertigo, or a Contemplation of Things that Come to an End"] in *Extracción de la piedra de locura* (1968): "This lilac unleaves. / It falls from itself / and hides its ancient shadow. / I will die of such things." Alejandra Pizarnik, *Extracting the Stone of Madness: Poems 1962-1972*. Trans. Yvette Siegert (New York: New Directions, 2016). French in original.

The Incarnate Word

First published in *Sur* 294 (May-June 1965). Republished in Antonin Artaud, *Texto*s [*Texts*] (Buenos Aires: Acuario, 1972) and in *El deseo de la palabra*.

Epigraph — "*Moi je reproche aux hommes de ce temps, de m'avoir fait naître par les plus ignobles manœuvres magiques dans un monde dont je ne voulais pas, et de vouloir par des manœuvres magiques similaires m'empêcher d'y faire un trou pour le quitter. J'ai besoin de poésie pour vivre, et je veux en avoir autour de moi. Et je n'admets pas que le poète que je suis ait été enfermé dans un asile d'aliénés parce qu'il voulait réaliser au naturel sa poésie.*" Antonin Artaud, *Lettres de Rodez* [*Letters from Rodez*], in *Antonin Artaud: Selected Writings*. Ed. Susan Sontag. Trans. Helen Weaver (Berkeley and Los Angeles: UC Press, 1976). Excerpted from a letter to Henri Parisot (October 6, 1945). French in original.

André Gide's testimony — André Gide, "Antonin Artaud," *Revue 84*, n. 5/6 (1948).

L'Alchimiste — The Alchemist

"Letter of a Seer." — "Lettre du Voyant." Two of Rimbaud's letters are identified as "Letters of the Seer," the first to Georges Izambard (Charleville, May 13, 1871) and the second to Paul Demeny (Charleville, May 15, 1871).

"The New Revelations of Being" — "Les Nouvelles Révélations de l'Etre" (1937). French in original.

"The Umbilicus of Limbo *and* Nerve Meter" — *L'Ombilic de Limbes* and *Le Pése-Nerfs*. French in original.

I entered the world of literature writing ... of Limbo *and* Nerve Meter. — Artaud, letter to Peter Watson (1946).

"I don't believe the most urgent ... as that of hunger." — Artaud, "Préface: Le théâtre et la culture" ["Preface: The Theater and Culture"], in *Le Théâtre et son Double* [*The Theater and its Double*] (1938).

Chinese Thought — *La Pensée Chinoise* (1934). French in original.

"To know the name, to say ... I call them: 'tigers!'" — "Savoir le nom, dire le mot, c'est posséder l'être ou créer la chose. Toute bête est domptée par qui sait la nommer... J'ai pour soldats des tigres si je les appelle: 'tigres!'" Marcel Granet, *La Pensée Chinoise,* 1934. French in original.

The main works of the "black period" are — Pizarnik cites the original French titles: *Au Pays des Tarahumaras*; *Van Gogh, le suicidé de la société*; *Lettres de Rodez*; *Artaud le Mômo*; *Ci-git précédé de la Culture Indienne*; and *Pour en finir avec le jugement de dieu*.

"to a degree that is unique in the history of literature." — Arthur Adamov, "L'Œvre indéfinissable d'Antonin Artaud" ["The Indefinable Work of Antonin Artaud"]. *Revue K*, n. 1/2 (June 1948).

"kind of phonetic miracle that ceaselessly renews itself." — Ibid.

"humanity's abhorrent misery" — André Gide, "Antonin Artaud."

"returning to Antonin Artaud after his ten years ... last one worth deciphering" — "...regagner Antonin Artaud sur ses dix ans de souffrances, pour commencer a entrevoir ce qu'il voulait dire, ce que veut dire ce signe jeté parmi nous, le dernier peut-être qui vaille d'être déchiffré..." Pizarnik quotes Marthe Robert's note on Artaud in *Revue 84*, n. 5/6 (1948). French in original.

Michaux's *Passages*

Five typed pages, hand-corrected by Pizarnik and an unidentified hand. At the top of the first page, Pizarnik's handwritten indication: "*El Nacional*, Caracas, 1964."
First published in *Prosa completa*.

This essay refers to Henri Michaux's *Passages* (Paris: Gallimard, 1963). Pizarnik's quotations from *Passages* appear in italics.

Illicit Domains

Dated 1967.
First published in *Sur* 311 (March-April 1968). Republished in *El deseo de la palabra*.

The focus of this piece is Silvina Ocampo's collection of stories, *El pecado mortal* [*The Mortal Sin*] (Buenos Aires: Eudeba, Serie de los contemporáneos, 1966). Pizarnik's quotations from Ocampo's stories appear in italics.

"There are certain looks of such complicated subtlety…" — Pizarnik is likely thinking of this passage from *A Sentimental Journey* (1768): "There are certain combined looks of simple subtlety—where whim, and sense, and seriousness, and nonsense, are so blended, that all the languages of Babel set loose together could not express them…"

"sacred and illicit domain" — This unattributed phrase—ostensibly a quotation—prefigures a line from Pizarnik's 1969 prose poem "Los muertos y la lluvia" ["The Dead and the Rain"]: "Solamente escucho mis rumores desesperados, los cantos litúrgicos venidos de la tumba sagrada de mi ilícita infancia" ["All I hear are my hopeless murmurings, liturgical chants that rise from the sacred tomb of my illicit childhood"].

Chango — In Argentina, "chango" is a familiar designation for "boy."

the school of voyeurism — *l'école du voyeurisme*. French in original.

"This man makes his doll laugh." — "L'homme fait rire sa poupée." Léon-Paul Fargue, *Tancrède* (1911). French in original.

La Celestina — *La Celestina* (1499) is the only surviving work of Spanish converso author and dramatist Fernando de Rojas.

"oyeuse" — hearer (female). Pizarnik's coinage. "French" in original.

"(…) **I don't think we … than Rodion Raskolnikov.**" — Alejandra Pizarnik and Ivonne A. Bordelois, "Interview with Jorge Luis Borges." *Zona Franca* 2 (1964).

Wise Men and Poets

Dated 1967.
First published in *Sur* 206 (May-June 1967). Republished in *El deseo de la palabra*.

Pizarnik refers to Enrique Anderson Imbert's collection of short stories, *El gato de Cheshire* [*The Cheshire Cat*] (Buenos Aires: Losada, 1965). Pizarnik's quotations from the collection appear in italics.

Enrique Anderson Imbert (1910-2000) — An Argentine fiction writer and critic, best known for his fantastic "microcuentos" ["microstories"].

The Humor of Borges and Bioy Casares

Seven typewritten pages, undated.
First published in *Prosa completa*.

This essay responds to Sur's 1971 reissue of Adolfo Bioy Casares and Jorge Luis Borges's pseudonymous collaboration, *Seis problemas para don Isidro Parodi* [*Six Problems for Don Isidro Parodi*] (Buenos Aires: Sur, 1941, 1971). Pizarnik's quotations from the book appear in italics.

compadritos — In Argentina, "compadrito" is a disparaging term for an affected, swaggering rabble-rouser or bully.

A Tradition of Rupture

First published in *La Nación* (Buenos Aires, November 26, 1966).

This review offers a detailed commentary on Octavio Paz's essay collection *Cuadrivio* (Mexico: Joaquín Mortiz, 1965). Pizarnik's quotations from the book appear in italics.

"and very eighteenth-century / and very modern, / audacious, cosmopolitan…" — Pizarnik refers to the opening poem of Rubén Darío's *Cantos de vida y esperanza* [*Songs of Life and Hope*] (1905):

> and very eighteenth-century and very ancient
> and very modern; bold, cosmopolitan;
> with Hugo strong and Verlaine ambiguous
> and an infinite thirst for illusion…

"To have gathered from the air a live tradition" — English in original.

Love your rhythm and rhythm your actions — In Spanish, the line reads: "Ama tu ritmo y ritma tus acciones." Rubén Darío, *Prosas profanas y otros poemas* [*Profane Hymns and Other Poems*] (1896).

"Uruguayan, never French" — The expression is Federico García Lorca's. Pizarnik's note.

If Rubén Darío *is modernismo* … any particular style. — See Octavio Paz, *El arco y la lira* [*The Bow and the Lyre*] (Mexico: Fondo de Cultura Económica, 1956). Pizarnik's note.

"musician of silence" — "Musicienne du silence." Stéphane Mallarmé, "Sainte" ["Saint"] (1865). French in original.

"the race that creates life with Pythagorean numbers" — Pizarnik refers to the epigraph that begins Paz's essay on Darío, taken from his sonnet "A Juan Ramón Jiménez" ["To Juan Ramón Jiménez"] (1900).

"the awareness of our human clay" — Pizarnik refers to the first of the three poems entitled "Nocturno" ["Nocturne"] in Darío's *Cantos de vida y esperanza*. The full line reads: "la conciencia espantable de nuestro humano cieno" ["the appalling awareness of our human clay"].

"between I am and you are, / the word *bridge*" — Ocavio Paz, "El Puente" ["The Bridge"] in *Salamandra* [*Salamander*] (Mexico: Joaquín Mortiz, 1962).

lyric tradition — Pizarnik, following Paz, refers specifically to the Provençal "pactos," or pacts, a term which highlights the Troubador poets' conception of the love relation as a contract or covenant.

"In the Portuguese poet Fernando Pessoa, we ... space to give it its chances." — Nora Mitrani, "Poésie Liberté d'être." *Le Surréalisme, même* 2 (spring 1957). Pizarnik's note.

"Of course, I'm not sure if they're the ones that don't exist or if I'm the nonexistent one. In such cases, we shouldn't be dogmatic." — Fernando Pessoa, letter to Adolfo Casais Monteiro (January 13, 1935).

"What followed was the appearance of someone in me, someone I immediately named Alberto Caeiro. Pardon the absurdity of my statement: my master appeared in me." — Ibid.

"By the painful light of the factory's huge electric lamps / I feverishly write. / I write gnashing my teeth rabid before this beauty, / This beauty utterly unknown to the ancients" — Álvaro de Campos, "Ode Triunfal" ["Triumphal Ode"] (1915).

"Reis writes better than I, but with a purism I consider exaggerated" — Pessoa, letter to Adolfo Casais Monteiro.

"which is not called fortune, fame, or glory" — Luis Cernuda, "Si el hombre pudiera decir" ["If man could say"] in *Los placeres prohibidos* [*Forbidden Pleasures*] (1931).

A NOTE ON THE DESIGN

THE COVER DESIGN of *A Tradition of Rupture* is inspired by Barcelona-born artist Josep Pla-Narbona's cover for *El deseo de la palabra* (Ocnos, 1975) where some of the essays in this book appeared together with a selection of Pizarnik's poetry. In the epilogue to that collection Antonio Beyneto discusses the author's participation in the selection process, noting that Pizarnik initially wanted to include only poetry, but that he insisted on making a book in which she could be seen "as a whole." Pizarnik's participation is confirmed by several letters of 1972 in which she writes enthusiastically to Beyneto about the project as a whole and about her friend Martha Isabel Moia's input regarding the selections. Although Pizarnik did not live to see its publication, she calls it "our" book.

The Ocnos series was itself divided into a number of subseries—"Spanish and Latin American," "Classics," "Translations," etc. All the books in the "Spanish and Latin American" series had the same design by Pla-Narbona: a white circle inside a blue square. For our edition, we replaced the blue with the green from the cover of Pizarnik's second poetry book, *The Last Innocence* (1956).

A Tradition of Rupture is designed and typeset in Garamond to be of a series with three other books of Alejandra Pizarnik published in English translation by Ugly Duckling Presse: *Diana's Tree* (2014), *The Most Foreign Country* (2017), and *The Last Innocence / The Lost Adventures* (2019).